SWEET SMELL OF SUCCESS

SWEET SMELL OF SUCCESS

Clifford Odets
and
Ernest Lehman

from the novelette by
Ernest Lehman

faber and faber

First published in 1998
by Faber and Faber Limited
3 Queen Square London WC1N 3AU

Photoset by Parker Typesetting Service, Leicester
Printed in England by Clays Ltd, St Ives plc

A CIP record for this book
is available from the British Library
ISBN 0–571–19410–9

2 4 6 8 10 9 7 5 3 1

CONTENTS

INTRODUCTION

To be literal, *Sweet Smell of Success* began one summer in the late forties in a rented room in Provincetown on Cape Cod, Massachusetts. I would bicycle over there each morning from our summer cottage and sit over my Royal portable until 1 p.m., when I'd switch from writing to tennis playing for the rest of the day.

I was fooling around with my first attempt at a novel, based loosely on my three or four years in Manhattan as a Broadway press agent, dependent on and more than a little fearful of the powerful gossip columnists of the era – Walter Winchell, Dorothy Kilgallen, Louis Sobol, Danton Walker. I called my novel *You Scratch My Back* –, and by summer's end, I had two convictions: 1) I was never really going to finish the book, but 2) I had written enough material to take back to New York and rewrite into two short stories, which I soon published in *Collier's* and *Cosmopolitan*, respectively, as 'Hunsecker Fights the World' and 'It's the Little Things that Count'.

But out of that summer of failed novel writing and two successful short stories, I derived a powerful conviction that there lurked a vivid, authentic, dangerous, exciting novelette in the world of columnists and press agents that I had been exploring, based on my own experiences along night-time Broadway.

Immediately on returning to my Manhattan home base, I rented a little hotel room a few blocks away from the apartment and holed in every day for all the day, bringing into being the story of J. J. Hunsecker and Sidney Falco and Susan Hunsecker, a story that would one day become famous, and even more serendipitously, I came up with a title, 'The Sweet Smell of Success', which was to have an endless destiny of its own.

Cosmopolitan editor Herbert R. Mayes bought this, my first long-form fiction, with immense enthusiasm, but would not use a title with the word 'smell' in it. The novelette was published in 1952 as *Tell Me about it Tomorrow*. It caused a sensation on Broadway: I had dared to take on a feared and powerful columnist, no matter how well I had cloaked him in the guise of fiction. I tensed, awaiting columnar retaliation, but it never came. However, no Hollywood film studio would dare go near my novelette as a possible movie. The Hollywood giants felt even more vulnerable than did the lowly press agent turned fiction writer.

It was when Paramount Pictures, impressed by *Sweet Smell* and a follow-up published novella called *The Comedian*, summoned me and family to the West Coast in 1952, that I began to receive repeated pleas from the independent producers Hecht-Hill-Lancaster to let them have the film rights to my work, with me doing the screenplay and directing.

I balked. Let sleeping dogs lie.

And then, in the mid-fifties, the Hecht-Hill-Lancaster independents won many Oscars, including Best Picture, with their production of *Marty*. Impressed, I quickly developed a newfound larger respect which overwhelmed all my fears. Contracts were signed, work began, several difficult drafts of the screenplay were tortured out of my typewriter, and I went to New York to nail down some shooting locations.

It was when I returned to California that I was suddenly confronted with distributor United Artists's decision to drop me as director. They had just been bitten by another first-time director, Burt Lancaster, doing *The Kentuckian*. I was so disappointed I started developing a pain in the gut (not realizing how lucky I would eventually be with Alexander Mackendrick directing). Came the day when Burt Lancaster told me I'd have to go to New York to do some screenplay rewriting while they were shooting. 'First I'll have to see my doctor,' I said, 'to find out what this pain in the gut is.' They sedated me overnight in a hospital, shoved a sigmoidoscope up my rear, and then the doctor said: 'Your colon is a clenched fist. You're not going back to the picture. You're not going to do *any* picture. You're going away, out of the country.'

Two weeks later, lying on the sands of Tahiti, I suddenly sat up. Six thousand miles away, the picture was shooting, and I had forgotten all about it.

Clifford Odets had done some brilliant rewrites, Tony Curtis gave the performance of a lifetime, and today, forty years later, I bask in the reflected glory of the work so many others did to make *The Sweet Smell of Success* an historic film.

Ernest Lehman

Sweet Smell of Success

HECHT, HILL and LANCASTER
Present
BURT LANCASTER and TONY CURTIS
In
SWEET SMELL OF SUCCESS
Introducing
SUSAN HARRISON
A Norma-Curtleigh Productions Picture
Released through United Artists

CAST

J. J. HUNSECKER	Burt Lancaster
SIDNEY FALCO	Tony Curtis
SUSAN HUNSECKER	Susan Harrison
STEVE DALLAS	Marty Milner
FRANK D'ANGELO	Sam Levene
RITA	Barbara Nichols
SALLY	Jeff Donnell
ROBARD	Joseph Leon
MARY	Edith Atwater
HARRY KELLO	Emile Meyer
HERBIE TEMPLE	Joe Frisco
OTIS ELWELL	David White
LEO BARTHA	Lawrence Dobkin
MRS BARTHA	Lurene Tuttle
MILDRED TAM	Queenie Smith
LINDA	Autumn Russell
MANNY DAVIS	Jay Adler
AL EVANS	Lewis Charles

Produced by James Hill
Directed by Alexander Mackendrick
Screenplay by Clifford Odets and Ernest Lehman
From the Novelette by Ernest Lehman
Photography by James Wong Howe, A.S.C.
Art Direction by Edward Carrere
Music Scored and Conducted by Elmer Bernstein
Songs by Chico Hamilton and Fred Katz

Running time: 103 minutes

EXT./INT. GLOBE NEWSPAPER BUILDING NY – DUSK

A row of newspaper delivery trucks is lined up against the long loading bay, waiting for the edition. In the foreground a large clock establishes the time as 8.10 p.m. A rumbling noise warns the men to take their positions; a few seconds later the bales of newspapers come sliding down the spiral chutes onto the moving belts from which they are manhandled onto the trucks. Much noise and shouting.

The front truck moves out to the city street. As it does camera emphasizes the big poster on its side. The design features a large pair of spectacles with heavy rims – a trademark of Hunsecker. (It will later be seen as the masthead of the gossip column.)

'GO WITH THE GLOBE'
Read
J. J. HUNSECKER
'The eyes of Broadway'

EXT. BROADWAY – DUSK

The truck starts on its journey along Broadway. Some shots are of the vehicle moving through very heavy traffic (taken from a camera car). Others are from the inside of the truck; as it slows down, the delivery man tosses the heavy bundle of papers onto the sidewalk. Camera following the truck, holds it in foreground against the blazing electric signs of Broadway and Times Square.

EXT. BROADWAY – NIGHT (DUSK)

The south-east corner of the intersection of Broadway and 46th Street. Camera, fairly high, shoots north toward the impressive vista of electric signs silhouetted against the darkening sky. Very heavy traffic and crowded sidewalks. Camera descends toward the orange juice stand on the corner, passing the booth which sells souvenir hats. It moves through the congestion of chattering passersby, steadily approaching a smartly dressed young man, who stands at the counter of the orange juice stand. Oblivious of the hubbub around him, Sidney Falco is concerned only with his private problems. He turns sharply as a newspaper truck pulls up at the curb behind him; this is what he has been waiting for . . .

CLOSER ANGLE

The news truck delivery man tosses a bundle out onto the sidewalk beside a news stand.

DETAIL

The bundle of newspapers. It hits the sidewalk with a smack. Camera pulls back as Sidney Falco crosses the sidewalk. The owner of the news stand, Iggy, comes to pick up the bundle; he is a grizzled gnome with a philosophical sense of humour; Sidney snaps his fingers with impatience. Iggy wears spectacles and is clearly more or less blind, he has to grope for the cord that binds the papers.

IGGY
Aw, Lady, if I looked like you, I'd –

SIDNEY
C'mon . . . C'mon . . .

IGGY
(*recognizing Sidney's voice*)
Keep ya sweatshirt on, Sidney.

Majestically taking his time, Iggy lifts the bundle to his stand and cuts the cord.

Hey, Fresh, the *Globe* just came in – Hey, Sidney, want an item for Hunsecker's column? Two rolls get fresh with a baker! Hey, hot, hot, hot – etc.

Annoyed, Sidney throws him a dime, seizes a paper and returns briskly to the orange juice stand.

4

ORANGE JUICE STAND – NIGHT

*Sidney's place at the crowded counter has been taken by newcomers.
Rudely, he recovers his half-consumed glass of orange juice and
sandwich. He takes them further down the counter to a quieter corner at
which he can examine the paper. Camera moving with him, picks up
further snatches of overheard dialogue. We move close enough to see
Sidney's hands open the paper expertly at Hunsecker's column –
identifiable by the picture of the spectacled eyes. Over scene there is a
babble of off-stage dialogue.*

CLOSE-UP OF SIDNEY

*His face is sullen as his eyes run rapidly down the column. He is reacting
to a not unexpected disappointment.*

EXT. SIDNEY'S APARTMENT. BROADWAY – NIGHT

*Camera shoots west on 46th Street as Sidney comes down the side street
from the news stand in background. Irritably he jerks open the door of a
shabby entrance. As the glass door closes, Sidney is seen striding up the
stairs.*

FIRST FLOOR. OUTSIDE SIDNEY'S APARTMENT – NIGHT

*Beside the top of the stairs is the door to Sidney's office. On it there is a
cheaply printed cardboard sign which reads:*

SIDNEY FALCO

Publicity

*From inside comes the sound of desultory typing. Sidney comes up the
stairs two at a time and turns into the door.*

INT. SIDNEY'S APARTMENT – NIGHT

Sally is on the phone as Sidney strides in.

SALLY
Just a minute, Mr Weldon. I think . . .

Sidney vigorously indicates that he doesn't want to take the call.

5

(*to phone*)
I'm sorry. I thought that was Mr Falco returning. Yes, I'll tell him when he comes in. I know he's been trying to reach you.

She hangs up.

That's the third time he's called today.

SIDNEY
He wants me to break a leg?

SALLY
(*literally*)
No, an arm, he said. I told him you were sure the item would be in Mr Hunsecker's column in tomorrow's . . .

SIDNEY
(*interrupting, sharply*)
It isn't. I've just seen the early edition.

SALLY
But . . .

SIDNEY
But *what*?

SALLY
That makes five days in a row that Mr Hunsecker's cut you out of his column.

SIDNEY
May I rent you out as an adding machine?

He has begun to change his clothes.

Get me Joe Robard.

Sally goes back into the outer room.

Who else phoned?

SALLY
The renting agent and the tailor.

SIDNEY
Pay the rent. Let the tailor wait.

6

It won't leave much of a balance in the bank . . .
(*into phone*)
Mr Robard? Could you locate him?

Sidney, in a state of semi-undress, comes to take the phone from her.

SIDNEY
(*gloomily*)
Watch me run a fifty-yard dash with my legs cut off!

Very abruptly, he comes alive on the phone. A real laughing boy.

(*effusively*)
Sidney, Joe. How do you like it? I'm running out of alibis!
No, I asked Hunsecker to withhold the item, until he could
give it a fine, fat paragraph. The column was running over
and I didn't want you kissed off with just a line . . .

INT. ROBARD'S CLUB – NIGHT

*Robard is a stolid, secure man, balding and with a moustache. He has a
morose sense of humor. He is speaking from a telephone on a little desk
at the end of the bar. In background, the club is open, but there are few
customers as yet. Some recorded jazz is being played while the musicians
are still arriving, strolling past in background, depositing their overcoats
and music cases in the little closet assigned to them.*

ROBARD
(*in answer to Sidney*)
Of course.
(*he listens to protest from Sidney*)
What is this, Sidney, a kissing game? You're a liar – that's a
publicity man's nature. I wouldn't hire you if you *wasn't* a
liar. I pay you a C-and-a-half a week wherein you plant big
lies about me and the club all over the map.
(*pause*)
Yeah, I mean in that sense. But also in the sense that you are
a *personal* liar, too, because you don't do the work I pay you
for.

7

RESUME SIDNEY

Sally is watching him, unhappy on his behalf.

> SIDNEY
> (*into phone*)
> Now, wait a minute, Joe. When I saw J. J. last night he
> said . . .

But Robard has cut off. Sidney hangs up. A silence. Sally tries to be comforting.

> SALLY
> I wish I could help in some way, Sidney.

> SIDNEY
> (*aggressively*)
> Help me with two minutes of silence!

Sally, hurt, says nothing. Presently, he adds:

> Go home, Sally. It's late . . .

> SALLY
> I hate to see you like this –

Sidney is abruptly savage.

> SIDNEY
> (*with cruelty*)
> So what'll you do if I feel nervous? You'll open your meaty,
> sympathetic arms . . .?

> SALLY
> (*breaking down*)
> Sid . . . you got me so . . . I don't know what . . .

She is crying. Sidney feels uncomfortable. Not too generously, he relents:

> SIDNEY
> You ought to be used to me by now.

> SALLY
> (*pathetically*)
> I'm used to you . . .

SIDNEY
(*with a touch of bitterness*)

No. You think I'm a hero. I'm no hero. I'm nice to people where it pays me to be. I gotta do it too much on the outside, so don't expect me to kowtow in my own office. I'm in a bind right now with Hunsecker so –

Sally is silent, then speaks apologetically, while Sidney puts on his jacket, adjusting the pocket handkerchief; hastily he throws a few anti-acid tablets into his mouth, chewing.

SALLY

Maybe I'm dumb, but why is Mr Hunsecker trying to squeeze your livelihood away? What do you stand this kind of treatment for?

SIDNEY
(*balefully*)

What do you do when the sun gives you a burn? You take it, don't you? I'm in this business for my financial health, not the kicks. Hunsecker is a golden ladder to the places I wanna get!

SALLY

But, Sidney, you make a living – where do you want to get?

SIDNEY
(vehement and proud)
Way up high, Sam, where it's always balmy! Where no one
snaps his fingers and says, 'Hey, Shrimp, rack up those balls!'
Or, 'Hey, mouse, run out and get me a pack of butts!' I don't
want tips from the kitty – I sit in the big game and play with
the big players. *My* experience I can tell you in a nutshell, and
I didn't dream it in a dream: dog eat dog!
(lapsing)
In brief, from now on, Sally, the best of everything is good
enough for me . . .

*He wags around the room a moment, biting her with his eyes. She is
both nonplussed but stirred by his eloquence.*

SALLY

Goodness, Sidney, don't get me wrong – I'm not telling you
what to do. But I feel bad when Mr Hunsecker hurts you
and –

SIDNEY
(grimly)
Every dog has his day!
(going)
Lock up and leave the key.

*The phone rings. Sidney is dressed by now. As Sally goes for it, he
makes for the outer door.*

If that's for me, tear it up!

SALLY

Take a topcoat.

SIDNEY

And leave a tip in every hat-check room in town?

He is already gone as she picks up the phone.

SALLY

Sidney Falco's office . . . Oh, Miss Kay, he tried to reach you.

No, he's at the barbers now. No, that's held over till the
Tuesday column . . .

LAP DISSOLVE TO:

INT. ELYSIAN ROOM – NIGHT

*The quintet. As the dissolve clears, a clatter of polite applause greets the
end of a previous number. Camera is on the bandstand, moving
smoothly through the group of five musicians as the rhythm of a new
number is set up: first the leader (a guitarist) snaps his fingers, giving
the tempo to . . . the bass, who 'walks' with the beat, bringing in . . .
the drums, which start a quiet, insistent wire-brush background for . . .
the cello and the flute, whose introductory phrases set the stage for . . .*

STEVE DALLAS

*. . . the guitar, the leader again. It comes in after this short preamble
with the first statement of melody. (The tune has a faint echo of
significance because it is one of the themes of the film, already heard as
a phrase in the background score of the title music.) Camera lingers a
moment on Steve Dallas. He is a youth of pleasant, intelligent
appearance. He plays with the intent air of the contemporary jazz
musician who takes his work very seriously indeed and affects a much
greater interest in the music and his fellow musicians than in the
listening audience.*

SIDNEY

*A close shot. Sidney has just entered the club, strolling into the vestibule
near the entrance. He wears an expression of oddly unsuitable
antagonism, as he looks forwards . . .*

DALLAS

*Seen in long shot from Sidney's viewpoint. Camera moves to include
Sidney in foreground again. He turns as he is accosted by Rita, the
cigarette girl of the club. She is a pert creature, attractive and not
unaware of the fact.*

RITA

Don't you ever get messages, Eyelashes? I called you twice.

11

SIDNEY
(*irked*)
I've been up to here. Listen, honey, tell me something. You
know Susan Hunsecker . . .?
(*Rita nods*)
Has she been in? I mean lately, in the last coupla days . . .?

RITA
I don't think so.

SIDNEY
You're sure? Find out for me.

RITA
(*with a nod*)
Sidney, can I talk to you a minute?

*Rita wears an injured air. Sidney, preoccupied with other worries,
callously ignores it.*

SIDNEY
Is Frank D'Angelo around?

RITA
At the bar – Sidney . . .

But Sidney has moved away from her.

D'ANGELO

*He is at the bar, listening with satisfaction to the music, watching the
performers and studying the audience. Sidney comes up behind him. We
see Sidney's eyes flick from D'Angelo toward the bandstand and back
again. Then, as he takes the stool next to D'Angelo, he assumes a
different manner, a sulky resentment. D'Angelo sees Sidney.*

D'ANGELO
(*to the bartender*)
Joe, give my nephew a drink.

SIDNEY
(*sullen*)
Your nephew doesn't want a drink.

D'Angelo is still watching the quintet. The guitar can be heard again.

ANOTHER ANGLE

Shooting past D'Angelo and Sidney towards the bandstand.

D'ANGELO
That's a lollipop boy, that. The kid is only great.

SIDNEY
And with ten percent of his future, *you're* great, too, Frank.

D'Angelo looks quickly at Sidney, sensing the undercurrent. Then he turns his back on the musicians, remarking in a quiet tone.

D'ANGELO
Went over to Philly yesterday an' seen the folks . . . it's nice you send them the fifty a month . . .

SIDNEY
(*after a pause*)
See my mother?

D'ANGELO
(*shaking his head*)
I only had a few hours.

A glum moment. Frank sips his highball: Sidney lights a cigarette, animosity on his face.

Thanks for the publicity spread you got the boys for the benefit tomorrow.

SIDNEY
(*begrudgingly*)
Robard's my client. I did it for him and his club, not your boys.

Frank again notes Sidney's resentful manner. Sidney looks toward the musicians.

(*quietly*)
Frank, I think maybe you lied to me.

D'ANGELO
(quietly)

Looka, Sidney, you're my own sister's son, but where does that give you the right to call me a liar?

SIDNEY
(looking towards Steve)

You told me that your boy was washed up with Susie Hunsecker, didn't you?

D'ANGELO

Yeah, and it's the truth, to the best of my knowledge. And, frankly, I'm glad. For Steve's sake, I'm glad, not yours. I manage these boys and I got their best interests at heart. Steve shouldn't get mixed up with *no* bimbo at his age.

SIDNEY
(narrowly)

You told him that?

D'ANGELO

Not in those exact words – you know what a temper he's got.

A pause. Sidney is thinking.

SIDNEY

When do these hot-headed boys of yours go on the road?

D'ANGELO

Coupla weeks. For eight weeks.

SIDNEY

That's a nice tour. All booked?
(D'Angelo nodding)
When was Susie around here last?

D'ANGELO

Four, five nights ago. That's how I know the romance is off. Also Steve's in a very bad mood.

SIDNEY
(abruptly)

Listen, Frank, you'd better make sure you're telling me the truth.

14

D'ANGELO
(*annoyed*)
I don't like this threatening attitude. When it comes to it,
what the heck is it *your* business what they do, this boy and
girl . . .

RITA

*Locating Sidney, she comes up behind him. He turns away from
D'Angelo as she whispers to him. As she departs, Sidney turns back.*

SIDNEY
If you knew Hunsecker as well as I did, you might understand
why it's my business. Maybe you're walking around blind,
Frank, without a cane.

Sidney gets off his stool. Casually, but to effect, he adds:

. . . and in case you didn't know it, Susie Hunsecker's out
there on the back step right now.

He turns away, glancing toward Steve on the bandstand behind him.

D'ANGELO

He looks disturbed.

INT./EXT. BACKSTAGE AND COURTYARD

*From D'Angelo's point of view. Camera looks up at Steve. The quintet
is now reaching the end of the number, a driving rhythm of considerable
excitement. A waiter passes in foreground and the camera cranes back
through the curtained doorway to the backstage part of the club. This
movement is continued as we see some other employees, including Jerry
Wiggins, the intermission pianist, who is waiting in the corridor near the
fire exit. As he steps out of the door to discard a cigarette, camera again
continues its movement, craning back and downward into the little
courtyard. Here, it discovers the figure of a young woman who is
waiting in the shadow near the steps of the fire-escape, listening to the
music.*

CLOSER ANGLE

This is Susan Hunsecker. She wears an expensive mink coat. It is oddly in contrast with her personality; the face is sensitive and intelligent, but childlike and tragic. A girl in adolescence already burdened with problems beyond her capacity. Over scene, the music continues. Susan shifts her position, knowing that the session will soon be at an end and that the musicians will be coming backstage.

INT. ELYSIAN ROOM

Steve is playing the last bars of the number; the whole group now in unison.

QUINTET

The music comes sharply, dramatically to its finish. There is some applause. The boys relax. Steve reaches for the microphone and in the characteristically casual manner of the 'cool' musician, announces the end of the set, thanking the audience, identifying the quintet by name and introducing the intermission pianist. During this, Carson, Chico and Paul wander off the bandstand behind him.

EXT. BACKSTAGE AND COURTYARD

Chico, Paul and Carson come through to the corridor backstage. As they do so, Chico, glancing out of the open door, sees Susan in the courtyard. He goes out onto the fire-escape; Paul follows behind.

CHICO

Hi! Susie . . .

SUSAN

Hello, Chico. Paul.

CHICO
(*to Paul*)
Throw a rope round this chick while I go get Steve.

Chico goes swiftly back into the club. Paul remains with Susan. There is a momentary silence; Paul is embarrassed because Susan is. Susan makes an effort at conversation, she nods toward the club.

16

Full house . . .?

Packin' 'em in.

INT. CLUB

Steve has been trapped by an Intellectual Young Woman in spectacles, a much-too-earnest devotee of progressive jazz.

DEVOTEE

I'm terribly interested in jazz – *serious* jazz. You studied with Milhaud, didn't you? This is such an interesting fusion of the traditional, classical form with the new progressive style, I just wanted to ask you how you came to form the group . . .

CHICO

He comes through the curtains of the doorway, pausing as he sees that Steve is involved with the Intellectual Young Woman.

REVERSE ANGLE

Steve glances at Chico over the shoulder of the Intellectual Young Woman. Seeing that Chico has something to say to him, he wriggles out of the Young Woman's clutches by passing the buck to the unfortunate Fred Katz, who is descending from the bandstand behind him.

STEVE

Well, we just sort of got together.
(*turning to introduce Fred*)
Maybe if you ask Mr Katz . . . He writes the stuff, you know.

FRED
(*blankly*)

Huh?

RESUME CHICO

Steve joins Chico and they go through the curtains into the corridor outside.

CORRIDOR

Chico, smiling, explains:

> CHICO
>
> Don't waste your time there, man. You've got something
> better waiting outside . . .
>> (*as Steve looks at him*)
> Susie's out there.

> STEVE

*His reaction betrays some emotion. (Over scene the intermission pianist
has begun to play a blues number.) Steve moves a quick step towards
the door to the courtyard, then hesitates – almost as if he was afraid to
go out. He meets Chico's eye again.*

> STEVE
>
> What did she say . . .?

> CHICO

He is amused, but sympathetic.

> CHICO
>
> You proposed to her, not me.
>> (*slapping him on the back*)
> Go get your answer . . .

ALTERNATIVE VERSION OF THE ABOVE TWO SHOTS

> STEVE

*His reaction betrays some emotion. (Over scene the intermission pianist
has begun to play a blues number.) Steve makes a quick movement
towards the door to the courtyard, then hesitates. He turns to Chico, and
his face shows a rueful apprehension. He raises his hand and crosses his
fingers in the gesture which means 'let's hope it's going to be all right'.*

REVERSE ANGLE

*Chico grins with sympathy. He slaps Steve on the shoulder. Steve opens
the door and goes out.*

COURTYARD

Susan, waiting at the foot of the iron steps, turns as Steve comes out on the fire-escape above. Steve comes quickly down the steps towards her, slowing down when he gets a few paces away from her.

SUSAN

She looks up at Steve.

STEVE

A close shot. In his expression we read his mute enquiry . . .

RESUME SUSAN

Quite deliberately, with eyes moistened by love and affection . . . she nods.

REVERSE ANGLE

Great relief and happiness can be seen in the boy's face. After a moment, he moves to her and she to him. They embrace swiftly, hold each other close and then kiss with passion. Presently, when the kiss is over, Susan speaks softly.

SUSAN
(*in a whisper*)
Steve . . . I'll . . . I'll try to make a good wife.

Steve is still too choked with relief to speak. For answer, he clasps her more tightly to him. The beam of light which falls on the iron stairs behind them narrows and then is extinguished.

CORRIDOR

Paul has closed the door. Turning, he shares a look with the grinning Chico and Fred Katz who has managed to escape from the Intellectual Young Woman. Before there is time for either of them to make a remark, Sidney comes through the curtains from the club.

SIDNEY
Hi, fellows. Where's the Chief?

Sidney's manner is very friendly. But it is immediately apparent from the reaction of the other three boys that none of them likes Sidney. Fred is deliberately uncomprehending.

FRED

Who?

SIDNEY
(*who gets the point*)
Dallas. Is he around?

Chico's back is to the closed door which opens onto the courtyard. Chico nods in the opposite direction, toward the stairs.

CHICO
(*unhelpfully*)
Yeah, he's around somewhere. Upstairs, maybe.

SIDNEY
(*coldly, as he goes*)
Thanks.

COURTYARD

Steve and Susan are still embracing. Steve is exultantly proud and happy.

STEVE
(*incoherent*)
This is big, you know. Very big! Let's go out later, drink some firewater. With the boys. Fred can call Millie and –

SUSAN
Steve, I'd rather you didn't say anything for a day or two . . . until I tell my brother . . .

STEVE

His sobering reaction shows this is something important.

STEVE
(*gently*)
You haven't told him yet . . .

SUSAN

I'm telling him in the morning, after breakfast.

Turning her head, she makes a little gesture, an unconscious movement, putting her fingers to her brow as if feeling a headache.

STEVE

He isn't going to like it.

Susan says nothing. She looks at Steve, smiling; but the smile is not too confident.

You sure you don't want me to be with you . . .?

Susan stoutly shakes her head. Defensively she reassures Steve.

SUSAN

Steve, my brother isn't as bad as he's painted. He isn't perfect, but –

STEVE

But he isn't going to like this, Susie. And he makes *you* nervous, not me. No, I take that back – he makes *me* nervous, too. But I wouldn't give him a second thought if not for you.

The topic evidently makes Susan uneasy. In an effort to dismiss something that she does not want to think about, Susan puts her arms around Steve's neck again.

SUSAN

Let's forget him and –

But Steve is not so ready to change the subject.

STEVE

His stooge, Falco, is around – I saw him walk in.
(*soberly*)
He's been spying on me for weeks, Susie.

SUSAN

(*quickly, perhaps too quickly*)
Darling, I don't care – really I don't. Sidney's had a secret crush on me for years, but nothing we do is his business –

STEVE
(*gently insisting*)
But he could be reporting back to your brother, couldn't he?

SUSAN
(*pleading*)
Steve, dear, please forget all of this. What can it matter after tomorrow?

Now Steve responds. He grins, holds her closer.

STEVE
(*softly*)
I have a message for you; I love you.
(*kissing her lightly*)
May I dedicate the next number to you? . . . And the next, and the next. Every Sunday I'll buy you a new bonnet –

SUSAN
(*amused, but moved*)
If the stores are open –

STEVE
And on Monday, I'll take if off and stroke your light brown hair and –

SUSAN
And on Tuesday – Hasenpfeffer.

STEVE
(*abruptly grinning*)
How do you think I realized I love you?

SUSAN
I made you write a beautiful song . . .

STEVE
No, you had me eating that Chinese food! . . .

They laugh enjoyably; but then, as the camera moves, we realize that Sidney is there on the fire-escape above them; his manner is affable.

SIDNEY
Can more than two enjoy this joke . . .

(*to Susan*)

Hello, Susie, I didn't expect to find *you* here.

Steve says nothing. But he obviously resents the intrusion and finds it difficult to conceal the fact. Sidney comes down the fire-escape toward them.

Where's those glossy prints you promised? Tonight's the latest I can place them –

STEVE

(*barely polite*)

Well, thanks, anyway – let's forget it.

(*to Susan*)

It's cold out here, Susie.

Steve makes a move to lead Susan back inside. It is a gesture which appears to dismiss Sidney. Sidney chooses to take umbrage:

SIDNEY

(*lightly sarcastic*)

Let me apologize for getting you that press spread. It's been an honor to serve you gratis.

Steve turns to Sidney; his manner is quiet but challenging.

STEVE

(*levelly*)

I get the feeling, Falco, that you're always snooping around . . .

SUSAN

(*quickly intervening*)

Steve, stop it please . . .

ANOTHER ANGLE

Frank D'Angelo has followed Sidney out onto the fire-escape; other members of the quintet have also appeared.

D'ANGELO

What are you boys fighting about?

Aggressively indignant, Sidney throws up his hands; he knocks on the metal of the fire-escape.

SIDNEY
(*sarcastic*)
Kill me! Find me a door somewhere – I walked in without
knocking!

*Sidney is trying to needle Steve; Steve's temper would normally have
exploded; but now he controls it.*

STEVE
I'm feeling too good to fight with you, but that isn't what I
said – I said you snoop. For instance, what were you doing
around my hotel the other night?

SIDNEY
(*needling*)
Begging your pardon, I haven't been down the bowery in
years!

D'ANGELO
(*soothingly*)
Come on boys, break it up . . .

STEVE
(*overriding D'Angelo*)
The next time you want information, Falco, don't scratch for
it like a dog – ask for it like a man!

SIDNEY

*His face tightens; he appears to be mortally insulted and controlling
himself with difficulty. He turns his back swiftly on Steve, addressing
Susan in a voice that has a sharp edge.*

SIDNEY
If you're going home, Susie, I'll drop you off . . .

*Sidney starts quickly up the fire-escape. This makes Steve angry and he
steps forward to follow him. But Chico contrives, without seeming to
interfere, to obstruct Steve.*

CHICO
(*easily*)
Time for the next set, Chief . . .

Just a minute, Chico.

CORRIDOR

Sidney comes inside. When he is out of sight of the group in the courtyard, his manner swiftly changes. It's obvious now that his indignation was assumed; now he looks back toward the courtyard and there is shrewdness in his eyes; he is assessing Steve's temper. But, presently, seeing D'Angelo and the boys returning, he moves back to the curtains and into the club.

COURTYARD

As D'Angelo and the other boys go inside, Steve turns back to Susan.

STEVE
(*fondly*)
Just so you don't leave me in a minor key.

INT. CLUB

Rita has succeeded in recapturing Sidney near the entrance to the club. Sidney, alert and interested, listens to her while keeping his eye on the bandstand in background where the intermission pianist is finishing his performance and the quintet are returning, ready to mount the bandstand again.

SIDNEY
Don't tell me you started a polka with Leo Bartha?

RITA
(*shaking her head*)
No. That's what I mean – I'm being fired for what I *didn't* do.

Sidney is amused. Rita continues in a confidential manner which is heavily loaded with sex appeal and not-very-convincing air of injury.

(*sotto voce*)
He came in last week on a very dull rainy night. I knew who he was, but I didn't let on.
(*emphatically*)
He didn't take his eyes off me all night. Listening . . .?

Rita has mistaken Sidney's shrewdly calculating expression for inattention.

SIDNEY

Avidly. He was staring.

RITA
(*continuing*)

Staring. Consequently, when he approached me on his way out I wasn't surprised, but I didn't let on.

SIDNEY
(*prompting*)

He was writing a special Sunday piece on . . .?

RITA
(*nodding*)

. . . cigarette girls . . . And naturally –

SIDNEY

You were thrilled to be interviewed.
(*she nods*)
Were you 'interviewed'?

RITA

In his apartment –

SIDNEY

And where was his wife?

RITA

I don't know – it's a big apartment. But I wasn't interviewed. In fact, I was totally unprepared for what happened.

SIDNEY
(*grimacing*)

We're old friends, Chickie – quit it! A big columnist comes in this room without his ball-and-chain, and you make like a delicatessen counter! What did you *think* would happen in his house?

(*with a nod*)

But, Sidney darling, the man must be out of his mind – it
was only eleven o'clock in the morning!

Despite himself, Sidney chuckles; but she is distressed.

For a moment I was so taken aback that I said anything that
popped into my sleepy head. If I'm not mistaken, I even
ordered the man out of his own house.

*Sidney's eyes have been caught by something at the other end of the big
room.*

STEVE AND SUSAN

*From Sidney's viewpoint. Susan has come back into the club with Steve
and seems to be taking leave of him. She starts to walk through the club
on her way out.*

RESUME SIDNEY AND RITA

*Sidney, with half his attention on Susan and Steve, listens to Rita's
rueful protest.*

RITA
(*rapidly*)

He was furious and, by the time I could have put on a
Tropical Island mood, I was out on the streets! . . .
(*dolefully*)

That night Mr Van Cleve calls me into his office here. He's
got nothing against me, he says, but he can't afford to
antagonize columnists. I told him I still have Sonny at
military academy, but Van Cleve's made of ice . . .

*Aware that Sidney is moving to leave her so that he can catch Susan,
Rita detains him with an appeal:*

(*tentative*)

Do you think you could do something, Sidney?

SIDNEY
(*a quick nod*)
That's what I'm thinking, Rita. Maybe . . .

Rita is anxious to cement the offer. Delicately, she asks:

RITA
Do you still keep your key under the mat?

SIDNEY
(*eyeing her*)
Can you be there by two-thirty?

She drops her eyes, nods. Sidney pats her arm and is gone. She looks after him.

SIDNEY AND SUSAN

Sidney overtakes Susan at the front entrance in time to open the door for her. He has now reverted to another mood in which he appears to be sulking over the insult delivered to him by Steve. He goes out ahead of her.

BANDSTAND

The quintet are resuming their positions on the stand. Steve lingers a moment, his guitar already in his hand while he talks to D'Angelo.

STEVE
Frank, I don't want any secrets from you. I proposed to Susie tonight.

D'Angelo hides his feelings, asks:

D'ANGELO
Did she accept?

STEVE
You don't like it, do you? I think she will accept, but I'm not sure. She may be too dependent on her brother.

He mounts the bandstand.

D'ANGELO
(*solemnly*)
Lots of good people in this town are dependent on her brother . . .

Steve sits on the stool, quietly gives the beat to his group and begins at once the guitar opening of a very simple and lonely melody ('The Sage').

ANOTHER ANGLE

While D'Angelo watches him, the boy continues. Camera tracks slowly back through the club as the chatter and babble of the customers begins to diminish in appreciation of the quiet melancholy of the music.

OUTSIDE THE ELYSIAN ROOM

Susan is standing beside the poster which features Steve, listening to the music from inside the club. Sidney comes to join her. He is now pretending to be hurt.

SUSAN
You're touchy, Sidney – don't be so touchy . . .

SIDNEY
(*gruffly*)
I wasn't looking for a brawl. I came to bring him a present. Wanna bite to eat?

Susan shakes her head. She looks up as she hears the doorman's whistle off screen. Sidney moves forward to escort her to the taxi.

LONGER SHOT

They cross the sidewalk and get into the cab. It starts off and camera pans with it.

INSIDE CAB

Susan is relaxed, content but thoughtful. Sidney flicks her a quick, anxious look. Finally, gloomily:

SIDNEY

Feels like a Monday night, don't it . . .?

SUSAN
(*softly*)

Not to me. Sometimes, the world feels like a cage. Then
someone comes along and opens the door . . . and it's never
Monday night again . . .
(*turning to Sidney*)
I wish you and Steve could like each other.

SIDNEY
(*grimacing*)

We stick in each other's craw.

SUSAN

Yes, but why?

SIDNEY

Well, for one thing, he thinks J. J. is some kind of monster.

SUSAN

Quizzically, she studies Sidney.

SUSAN

Don't you?

SIDNEY

*He looks up sharply, he is momentarily startled at Susan's insight.
Swiftly, he assumes a protesting air.*

SIDNEY

Susie, your brother's one of my best friends, and –

RESUME SUSAN

She is not totally convinced by this performance. She smiles skeptically.

SUSAN

I know. But someday I'd like to look into your clever mind
and see what you *really* think of him –

RESUME SIDNEY AND SUSAN

Sidney makes a show of indignation.

SIDNEY

Where do you come off to make a remark like that?

SUSAN
(*quietly*)

Who could love a man who keeps you jumping through
burning hoops, like a trained poodle?

*Sidney doesn't answer immediately. Susan drops her eyes, becoming
absorbed in her own problems. Cautiously, Sidney lets the momentary
silence continue. Then:*

(*thoughtfully*)

Do you think J. J. likes Steve . . .?

SIDNEY
(*glibly*)

Frankly, yes, to my surprise. He thinks he's very gifted – those
boys'll go a big mile, he thinks.

Susan says nothing. Sidney, watching her closely, probes further.

(*gently*)

You feel pretty strong about this boy?

*A pause. Then Susan nods. She is not looking at Sidney and cannot see
the watchfulness in his face. Sidney prompts again.*

Wedding bells, you mean?

Again Susan nods.

SUSAN

He wants me to go on the road with them. It's an eight-
month tour, all the way to Oregon . . .

SIDNEY

*The news has considerable impact on Sidney. But he hides it, saying
lightly:*

31

SIDNEY

Well, congratulations. But don't go just for the ride! Or
didn't you accept the proposal?

RESUME SUSAN AND SIDNEY

Susan continues.

SUSAN

I'm going to discuss it with J. J. in the morning.

*A pause. Each is concerned with private thoughts. Susan, relaxed, adds
quietly:*

(*softly*)
It's given me a big lift to know that some people want me for
myself, not just because I'm my brother's sister.

SIDNEY

Chickie, I'll have to laugh at that – an attractive girl like
you . . .!

Susan ignores his remark, continuing thoughtfully:

SUSAN

I hope that J. J. really likes Steve, that it isn't an act.

SIDNEY

(*with an indignant edge*)
Why should he put on an act? Your brother has told *presidents*
where to go and what to do!

*The taxi has pulled to a stop. Susan sits for a moment before she
remarks:*

SUSAN

The act would be for my sake, not Steve's . . .

*Realizing that they have come to their destination, Susan gets up,
moving out of camera as she disembarks from the taxi. Camera catches
a glimpse of apprehension in Sidney's eyes. Quickly, he decides to follow
her.*

EXT. BROADWAY

Susan, getting out of the taxi, moves past camera. Sidney, following her, instructs the driver.

> SIDNEY
> (*to cabbie*)
> Wait for me. I'll be right back.

LONGER SHOT

Sidney moves after the girl, calling: 'Susie!'

SUSAN

Hearing him, Susan turns back. Sidney walks into shot to join her.

> SIDNEY
> (*lightly*)
> It's not my nature, Susie, but I'll talk to you like an uncle . . .

> SUSAN
> (*smiling*)
> But I don't need an uncle, Sidney.

They move through the doors.

REVERSE ANGLE

Sidney quickly corrects himself, saying earnestly:

> SIDNEY
> No, I mean because I admire you – in fact, *more* than admire you – although that's neither here nor there.
> (*quickly skipping to the important point*)
> Susie, don't sell your brother short. Talk this over with him, I mean – you'll find him a real friend.

SUSAN

Susan looks thoughtful, making no comment.

RESUME SIDNEY AND SUSAN

Carefully (again probing) he prompts her:

SIDNEY
Any message, in case I see J. J. later?

Susan turns away and walks out past camera. Sidney watches her.

SUSAN

She looks back at Sidney, quietly firm.

SUSAN
Yes. Tell him for me that Steve Dallas is the first real man
I've ever been in love with . . .

*She turns away and walks through the inner door, going down the
corridor towards the elevators in background.*

RESUME SIDNEY

*The sincerity of the girl's manner strikes home to Sidney. Now that her
back is turned we see the sharp twinge of pain with which he hears the
statement of her feelings for another man. Angered, he wheels, striding
out of the door onto Broadway.*

EXT. BROADWAY

Sidney returns to the cab, instructing the driver:

SIDNEY
The Twenty-One Club.

He climbs in and the taxi drives off down Broadway.

LAP DISSOLVE TO:

EXT. TWENTY-ONE CLUB – NIGHT (DUSK)

*Camera high, shooting west down 52nd Street, as Sidney's cab pulls up,
double parking in front of the Twenty-One Club. Sidney maneuvers his
way between the parked cars towards the entrance and the camera
descends to shoot along the courtyard toward the entrance. We see the
figure of Jimmy Weldon and his girlfriend coming out of the club.*

34

CLOSER ANGLE – NIGHT

Jimmy Weldon is coming out of the club accompanied by a girl; he is slightly tight. As he steps through the outer doors, Weldon again spies Sidney on the sidewalk; he steps to one side of the entrance way.

Sidney slips through the congestion, but just as he tries to enter the club, Weldon's hand shoots out, neatly ambushing him, pulling him aside into the narrow courtyard. Sidney is instantly resentful of this manhandling, but has to adjust himself, assuming a quick smile for the benefit of Weldon.

SIDNEY

Jimmy! This *is* a coincidence. I am just going –

WELDON
(overlapping)

Yeah. A coincidence you should run into the very man you've been ducking all week!

(to the girl)

This is my press agent, Joan.

Weldon, jibing at Sidney, plays his remarks off the girl, who is amused; Sidney, of course, is not.

SIDNEY
(quickly)

I tried to reach you twice –

WELDON
(overlapping)

What do you do for that hundred a week. Fall out of bed?

SIDNEY

Jimmy, I'm on my way inside right now to talk to Hunsecker. I can promise you –

WELDON
(horsing)

Joan, call a cop! We'll arrest this kid for larceny!

Sidney flinches, his pride touched.

35

SIDNEY
Listen, when your band was playing at Roseland –

WELDON
(*cutting in*)
That was two months ago. Take your hand out of my pocket,
thief!

*The girl tries to quiet Weldon, who has gone from horsing to loud
contempt.*

THE GIRL
Take it easy, Jimmy dear . . .

WELDON
(*indignantly*)
Why? It's a dirty job, but I pay clean money for it, don't I?

Abruptly Sidney bursts out, giving as good as he has taken:

SIDNEY
No more you don't! What is this – You're showing off for her?
They're supposed to hear you in Korea?

WELDON
(*smirking to the girl*)
He's intuitive – he knows he's getting fired!

SIDNEY
If you're funny, James, I'm a pretzel! Drop dead!

*Weldon, shepherded by the girl, is already on his way across the
sidewalk.*

WELDON
It was nice knowing you, Sidney. Not cheap – but nice.
Happy unemployment insurance.

INT. TWENTY-ONE CLUB – NIGHT

*Sidney, entering the club, threads his way through the crowded foyer,
coming up to camera near the foot of the staircase. There he meets a
Captain who turns to him.*

CAPTAIN

How are *you* tonight, Mr Falco?

SIDNEY

(*nodding towards the restaurant*)

Is 'he' inside?

CAPTAIN

But of course . . .

SIDNEY

Alone or surrounded?

CAPTAIN

A senator, an agent and something – with – long – red – hair.

Sidney moves past camera, coming a couple of paces toward the door to the restaurant. He pauses.

REVERSE ANGLE

From Sidney's viewpoint. Shooting through the doorway into the restaurant, we can see the group at the table. (Hunsecker's back is turned to us.) Camera pulls back to include Sidney in foreground. He decides not to go into restaurant and turns away out of shot.

INT. LOUNGE

Sidney comes round the corner from the foyer and walks through the lounge to the door into the alcove where the phone booths are, camera panning.

PHONE BOOTHS

Sidney moves briskly past the girl at the switchboard, instructing her:

SIDNEY

Honey, get me Mr Hunsecker.

The girl reaches for a book of phone numbers, then remembers:

OPERATOR

He's right inside, Mr Falco.

37

SIDNEY
(*from inside the booth*)
So it isn't long distance.

*As the girl, shrugging, puts through the call, camera moves closer to
Sidney in the booth. He hears the connection made, speaks at once.*

J. J., it's Sidney. Can you come outside for one minute?

*Hunsecker's voice, filtered through the sound of the telephone, is sharp
and tinny; but the words are now very clear.*

HUNSECKER'S VOICE
Can I come out? No.

SIDNEY
(*tensely*)
I have to talk to you, alone, J. J., that's why.

HUNSECKER'S VOICE
You had something to do for me – you didn't do it.

SIDNEY
Can I come in for a minute?

HUNSECKER'S VOICE
No. You're dead, son – get yourself buried!

*There is a click as Hunsecker hangs up. Sidney, more slowly, also hangs
up. Brooding, he comes out of the booth.*

INT. TWENTY-ONE CLUB. LOUNGE

*Sidney comes out of the door to the phone booths, walks through the
lounge to the hallway. He turns toward the dining room.*

INT. HALLWAY

*Sidney comes to the door into the dining room, camera tracking with
him. Here he pauses, looking towards . . .*

HUNSECKER

*From Sidney's viewpoint. Hunsecker is seated at a table which is clearly
his habitual position. We see him only in semi-back view, a broad and*

38

powerful back. He is listening to a man who has paused at his table, stooping over Hunsecker to whisper in his ear. As the columnist listens, his hands play with an omni-present pad and pencil which lie on the dinner table amongst an assortment of envelopes, mimeographed sheets and a telephone. Beyond Hunsecker and the man talking to him are the Senator, the Agent, and an attractive, if fatuous Girl.

HUNSECKER

I'll check it in the morning, Lew – thanks.

The man leaves; Hunsecker is scribbling a note on the pad. Meanwhile the Senator whispers something to the girl, who giggles softly.

REVERSE ANGLE

Sidney comes across to the table, nervous but deliberate. Camera pulls back to include Hunsecker in foreground. Sidney, without accosting him, stands a few feet from the columnist's elbow and deliberately lights a cigarette. Hunsecker, barely turning his head, sees him. We have heard of Hunsecker as a monster, but he is evidently in a mild phase of his metabolism, for he seems gentle, sad and quiet, as he turns his gaze casually to the Senator, totally ignoring the young man who stands behind him.

HUNSECKER
(*softly*)
Harvey, I often wish I were dead and wore a hearing aid . . .
with a simple flick of a switch I could shut out the greedy
murmur of little men . . .

SIDNEY

*A close shot. Sidney shows no reaction to this insult. He steps in closer,
an Indian fixity in his face.*

SIDNEY
J. J., I need your ear for two minutes . . .

REVERSE ANGLE

*Shooting across Sidney, onto Hunsecker. J. J. turns – but not to Sidney.
He raises his hand in a small gesture which summons a passing
Captain, who steps into picture at Sidney's elbow.*

HUNSECKER
Mac! I don't want this man at my table . . .

SIDNEY
(*quickly but quietly interrupting*)
I have a message from your sister.

*The Captain is already there. But now Hunsecker's eyes have switched
to Sidney's face. For the briefest of moments, nothing happens. Then
Hunsecker, seeming to relax and ignoring the Captain whom he has
summoned, turns back to casual conversation with the Senator as if
nothing had happened.*

HUNSECKER
Forgive me, Harvey. We were interrupted before –

*In foreground, Sidney turns to the Captain with a carved smile,
indicating that Hunsecker's change of topic is to be interpreted as
sanction for Sidney to remain. The Captain, not entirely convinced,
retreats. Sidney finds himself a chair, places it and takes a seat which is
near enough to the table to establish his presence. During this:*

SENATOR
(*who is mildly surprised and faintly embarrassed*)
Err . . . the Supreme Court story, I was telling you – Justice
Black.

HUNSECKER
(*nodding*)
Yes, the Justice, that's right. But I think I had it in the
column.

SIDNEY
(*smoothly, casually*)
Last July, the lead item . . .

*Sidney's interjection is quietly well-mannered. Hunsecker totally ignores
it. The other members of the party are a little astonished at the interplay.
The girl, in particular, is fascinated; she clearly admires Sidney's looks.
The Senator, noting this, glances at Sidney, accepting the point:*

SENATOR
(*laughing*)
And I believe that's precisely where I read it, too. You see,
J. J., where I get my reputation for being the best-informed
man in Washington.

HUNSECKER
Now don't kid a kidder.

THE SENATOR, THE GIRL, AND THE AGENT

*The girl looks again towards Sidney. The Senator again sees this,
addresses Sidney pleasantly:*

SENATOR
I don't think we caught your name, young man.

REVERSE ANGLE

*Group shot. The Senator in foreground, Sidney beyond Hunsecker in
background, and the others on edge of shot.*

SIDNEY
Sidney Falco, sir. And, of course, everyone knows and
admires *you*, Senator Walker.

41

SENATOR
(*humorously*)
Every four years I get less convinced of that. This young lady
is Miss Linda James.
(*indicates the Girl*)
She's managed by Manny Davis.
(*he indicates the Agent*)

SIDNEY AND HUNSECKER

Sidney nods pleasantly to the Girl and the Agent.

SIDNEY
I know Manny Davis.

HUNSECKER
(*quietly*)
Everyone knows Manny Davis . . .
(*as the phone rings on the table*)
. . . except *Mrs* Manny Davis.

Hunsecker is picking up the phone, continuing:

Yes? Go ahead, Billy – shoot . . .

REVERSE ANGLE

To intercut with the above. The Senator, the Agent and the Girl watching Hunsecker. The Agent's reaction to Hunsecker's remark is a sickly smile.

RESUME HUNSECKER

He repeats aloud a story which is told him over the telephone.

Uh huh. Sports cars in California are getting smaller and smaller . . . the other day you were crossing Hollywood Boulevard and you were hit by one . . . you had to go to the hospital and have it removed . . .
(*coolly*)
You're not following the column: I had it last week.

During the speech, camera eases back to include Sidney again. At the end, Sidney looks up in the direction of the Senator.

SIDNEY
Do you believe in capital punishment, Senator?

RESUME REVERSE ANGLE

The Senator, amused, asks:

SENATOR
Why?

RESUME HUNSECKER AND SIDNEY

Sidney glances sidelong at Hunsecker.

SIDNEY
(*pointing to the phone*)
A man has just been sentenced to death . . .

Hunsecker's face hardens; aware of Sidney's impertinence, he does not deign to react directly; he turns toward the Agent.

HUNSECKER

Manny, what exactly are the unseen gifts of this lovely young thing that you manage . . .?

THE AGENT AND THE GIRL

The Agent glances uneasily at the Girl beside him.

AGENT

Well, she sings a little . . . you know, sings . . .

GIRL
(*by rote*)

Manny's faith in me is simply awe-inspiring, Mr Hunsecker. Actually, I'm still studying, but –

RESUME HUNSECKER

He studies the Girl intently.

HUNSECKER

What subject?

RESUME THE AGENT AND THE GIRL

GIRL

Singing, of course . . . straight concert and –

RESUME HUNSECKER

Hunsecker's glance flicks between the Girl and the Senator.

HUNSECKER

Why 'of course'? It might, for instance, be politics . . .

As the Girl betrays herself with a nervous glance at the Senator beside her, camera eases back to include him. The Senator is unruffled; gravely, he lights a cigar. The Girl laughs.

GIRL

Me? I mean 'I'? Are you kidding, Mr Hunsecker? With my Jersey City brains?

RESUME HUNSECKER

Again his glance links the Girl and the Senator.

> HUNSECKER
>
> The brains may be Jersey City, but the clothes are Trainor-Norell.

THE SENATOR, THE AGENT AND THE GIRL

The Girl and the Agent are both nervously uneasy. The Senator closely examines the tip of his cigar and, with deliberation, turns toward Sidney.

> SENATOR .
>
> Are you an actor, Mr Falco?

> GIRL
> *(supporting the change of subject)*
> That's what *I* was thinking. *Are* you, Mr Falco?

SIDNEY AND HUNSECKER

Hunsecker, for the first time, half-turns in Sidney's direction, amused.

> HUNSECKER
>
> How did you guess it, Miss James?

RESUME THE AGENT, THE GIRL AND THE SENATOR

They all look at Sidney.

> GIRL
>
> He's so pretty, that's how.

RESUME SIDNEY AND HUNSECKER

Sidney bitterly resents the adjective, but contrives to hide the fact; he smiles, gracefully accepting the compliment. Hunsecker (who knows what Sidney feels) is pleased; he turns toward Sidney expansively.

> HUNSECKER
>
> Mr Falco, let it be said at once, is a man of forty faces, not one, none too pretty and all deceptive. See that grin? It's the

charming street urchin's face. It's part of his 'helpless' act – he throws himself on your mercy. I skip the pleading nervous bit that sometimes blends over into bluster. The moist grateful eye is a favorite face with him – it frequently ties in with the act of boyish candor: he's talking straight from the heart, get it? He's got about half a dozen faces for the ladies, but the real cute one to me is the quick dependable chap – nothing he won't do for you in a pinch. At least, so he says! Tonight Mr Falco, whom I did not invite to sit at this table, is about to show in his last and most pitiful role: pale face with tongue hanging out. In brief, gentlemen and Jersey Lilly, the boy sitting with us is a hungry press agent and fully up on all the tricks of his very slimy trade!

Hunsecker has started his speech lightly, but it has built up to enough cold contempt and feeling to embarrass and intimidate the others at the table. In conclusion, Hunsecker, his eyes on Sidney, picks up a cigarette and waits expectantly . . .

HUNSECKER
(*quietly*)

Match me, Sidney . . .

SIDNEY
(*coolly*)

Not just this minute, J. J. . . .

Amused, Hunsecker lights his own cigarette, turns toward a man who comes up to the table.

HUNSECKER

A single close-up, to intercut with the above.

SIDNEY

A matching single; Sidney's reaction to Hunsecker and to the others at the table.

THE AGENT, THE GIRL AND THE SENATOR

To intercut with the above; their reactions of embarrassment.

46

A florid man comes up to the table, obviously anxious to catch Hunsecker's attention. Hunsecker, in the act of lighting his own cigarette, scarcely looks at the man as he dismisses him:

> HUNSECKER
> I know – that loafer of yours opens at the Latin Quarter next week.
> *(more sharply)*
> Say goodbye, Lester!

The florid man retreats. To cover the embarrassment, the Senator makes a sally in Sidney's direction.

> SENATOR
> May I ask a naive question, Mr Falco? Exactly how does a press agent work . . .?

SIDNEY AND HUNSECKER

Sidney doesn't answer.

> HUNSECKER
> Why don't you answer the man, Sidalee? He's trying to take you off the hook.

> SIDNEY
> *(to the Senator)*
> You just had a good example of it. A press agent eats a columnist's dirt and is expected to call it manna.

RESUME THE AGENT, THE GIRL AND THE SENATOR

> GIRL
> What's manna?

RESUME HUNSECKER AND SIDNEY

Hunsecker glances spitefully at the Girl.

> HUNSECKER
> Heaven dust.

47

RESUME THE AGENT, THE GIRL AND THE SENATOR

The Senator continues to Sidney:

SENATOR
But don't you help columnists by furnishing them with items?

RESUME SIDNEY AND HUNSECKER

Sidney leans forward, indicating to the Senator some of the items of paper that litter the table in front of Hunsecker; these are both handwritten notes and mimeographed sheets, scraps of assorted items from professional and amateur agents who supply the columnist. Sidney fingers some of them.

SIDNEY
Sure, columnists can't get along without us. Only our good and great friend, J. J., forgets to mention that. We furnish him with items –

Sidney lifts a mimeographed sheet, as an example.

HUNSECKER
What, some cheap, gruesome gags?

SIDNEY
(*to Hunsecker now*)
You print them, don't you?

HUNSECKER
Yes, with your clients' names attached. That's the only reason those poor slobs pay you – to see their names in my column all over the world! Now, as I make it out, you're doing *me* a favor!

SIDNEY
I didn't say that, J. J.

HUNSECKER
The day that I can't get along without press agents' handouts, I'll close up shop, lock, stock and barrel and move to Alaska.

THE AGENT, THE GIRL AND THE SENATOR

The Agent makes the mistake of trying to agree with Hunsecker.

48

AGENT
(*nodding*)
Sweep out my igloo, here I come.

Camera pulls back as Hunsecker leans forward across the table. He vents upon the unfortunate Agent some of the annoyance prompted by Sidney's impertinence.

HUNSECKER
(*to the Agent*)
Look, Manny, you rode in here on the Senator's shirt-tails, so shut your mouth!

The Senator doesn't like this treatment of others and his manner and face show it.

SENATOR
(*slowly*)
Now, come, J. J., that's a little too harsh. Anyone seems fair game for you tonight.

HUNSECKER
(*not as harsh, but –*)
This man is not for you, Harvey, and you shouldn't be seen with him in public. Because that's another part of a press agent's life – he digs up scandal among prominent men and shovels it thin among the columnists who give him space.

SENATOR

He finds Hunsecker's manner disturbing, but addresses him frontally.

SENATOR
There is some allusion here that escapes me . . .

HUNSECKER

HUNSECKER
(*an edge of threat*)
We're friends, Harvey – we go as far back as when you were a fresh kid congressman, don't we?

49

RESUME SENATOR

Why does everything you say sound like a threat?

RESUME HUNSECKER

He leans back, speaking more quietly, enjoying himself.

Maybe it's a mannerism – because I don't threaten friends,
Harvey. But why furnish your enemies with ammunition?
You're a family man. Someday, with God willing, you may
wanna be President. Now here you are, Harvey, out in the
open where any hep person knows that this one . . .

AGENT

Hunsecker leans into shot pointing directly at the Agent.

(*continuing*)
. . . is toting *that* one . . .

*Hunsecker points to the Girl and the camera makes a slight crab
movement to include the Girl as Hunsecker points in turn to her.*

(*continuing*)
. . . around for *you* . . .

*Another camera movement. Now Hunsecker is directly challenging the
Senator.*

RESUME HUNSECKER

He smiles disarmingly.

(*continuing*)
. . . Are we kids or what? . . .

Hunsecker rises.

GROUP SHOT

As Hunsecker stands up, Sidney follows suit. The Agent, very nervous,

*gets to his feet and the Girl does likewise. The Senator, whose face is
sober, also rises from the table.*

> HUNSECKER
> (*to the Senator, affably*)
> Next time you come up, you might join me at my TV show.

*With Sidney making way for him, Hunsecker walks round the end of
the table to the Senator. The Senator faces Hunsecker solemnly.*

> SENATOR
> (*quietly and cautiously*)
> Thank you, J. J., for what I consider sound advice.

Hunsecker matches the Senator's solemnity.

> HUNSECKER
> (*deadpan*)
> Go, thou, and sin no more.

*Hunsecker moves out of shot. Sidney murmurs a 'pleased to meet you' to
the Senator; then he follows Hunsecker. The Senator remains looking
after Hunsecker. Behind him, the Agent and the Girl watch him
apprehensively. The Senator, his face now showing the traces of guilt
which he did not reveal to Hunsecker, seems unwilling to turn back to
face them.*

ON THE WAY TO THE FOYER

*Hunsecker and Sidney. Hunsecker addresses the Captain on his way out
of the restaurant.*

> HUNSECKER
> Mac, don't let the Senator pay that check . . .

> CAPTAIN
> I'll take care of it, Mr Hunsecker.

*Camera tracks with Hunsecker and Sidney as they move out toward the
hat check stand.*

> HUNSECKER
> (*murmuring*)
> President! My big toe would make a better President!

By now they are at the coatroom, Hunsecker smiling.

ATTENDANT
Mr Hunsecker's coat, Joe.

HUNSECKER
Find me a good one, Joe.

He accepts the proffered coat as he moves past camera.

LONGER SHOT – NIGHT

The Doorman on the sidewalk has noticed Hunsecker, almost before the columnist has appeared. The Doorman wheels, snapping his fingers and signalling toward the car park attendant, who can be seen at some distance in the background under the lights of the Kinney Car Park. The attendant is seen to react with alacrity, running into the park.

HUNSECKER

Putting on his overcoat, he addresses another of the Captains who has escorted him out of the club.

HUNSECKER
Dan, anyone calls, tell 'em I'll be at El Morocco, maybe the Embers.

DAN
Very good, Mr Hunsecker.

Sidney catches up with Hunsecker as he moves out onto the sidewalk.

HUNSECKER
Where's your coat, Sidalee? Saving tips?

Sidney thinks of an impertinent reply, decides not to be drawn and says nothing.

(*to Sidney*)
My curiosity is killing me; what are you so rambunctious about tonight?

Sidney again does not answer; this time he points across the street . . .

SIDNEY
There's your fat friend.

EXT. LONGER SHOT. POLICE CAR – NIGHT

The car is framed in foreground; we can read the sign POLICE *attached to the visor. Two men in plain clothes, detectives, are in the front seats. The man nearest is Harry Kello. Wanting to look like a prosperous businessman, Kello looks soft, fat, mild and well-barbered; but he is dangerous; he knows it and enjoys it. With 'big shots' he is playful and kidding, always says just enough, not too much. He is very relaxed, and mild in manner, but underneath there is not only an animal energy, but a feral energy pressing at you. His voice is on the hoarse side. He measures situations automatically and instantly.*

The police radio is chattering. Also in evidence is the telephone – the radio link with headquarters. The detective at the wheel nudges Kello, pointing across the street. Kello gets out of the car and moves to meet the columnist.

> HUNSECKER
> (*as he approaches*)
>
> Hello, Harry.

> KELLO
> (*cheerfully*)
> Buonasera, commendatore. Come sta?

Sidney follows a couple of paces behind Hunsecker; he is in no hurry to meet the detective, whom he clearly dislikes.

> HUNSECKER
> (*turning to Sidney*)
> You see, Sidalee, that shows that Lieutenant Kello likes your people.

REVERSE ON KELLO

Kello offers his hand to Hunsecker.

> KELLO
> It's my Brooklyn background, J. J. I'm good on Yiddish, too.

Hunsecker accepting the handshake, winces with pretended pain at what is clearly an over-enthusiastic grip.

HUNSECKER
Harry, am I supposed to say 'uncle'?

Kello laughs, releases the grip; Hunsecker strolls past him and stoops to lean into the car, listening to the police calls on the radio.

(*to the policeman in the car*)
Hello, Phil. How're the kids?

The detective inside the car answers, respectfully.

PHIL
Fine, Mr Hunsecker.

HUNSECKER
Any news fit to print tonight?

KELLO
(*joining Hunsecker*)
I just checked 'downtown'. Quiet everywhere tonight.

HUNSECKER
Incidentally, what happened to that doll? – You gave me the item last night. Still alive?

KELLO
Yeah. At Bellevue. Still hanging on. But they still don't know if she was pushed.

HUNSECKER
She mighta jumped. Love suicide?
(*to the policeman in the car*)
Check it for me, Phil . . . it's a real heartthrob.

While Phil lifts the radio phone, calling headquarters, Hunsecker turns back to Kello and Sidney.

ANOTHER ANGLE

Mischievously, Hunsecker nods at Sidney.

HUNSECKER
(to Kello)

Say hello to Sidney Falco. Tickle him – he's been a bad boy tonight. He called you my fat friend.

KELLO
(mildly)

I don't believe it.

Instantly aware that J. J. is toying with Sidney, Kello offers his large hand to Sidney, who refuses it.

SIDNEY

I know . . . I know you're the strongest cop in town.

KELLO
(with a laugh)

I call him the boy with the ice-cream face!

HUNSECKER
(laughing)

Say, that's good – it's nice – in fact, it's *apt*, Harry!

KELLO
(modestly)

Yeah, I got eyes. I put things together.

HUNSECKER

I remember *once* when you didn't quite 'put things together'. Boy! Was the Mayor mad!

The memory of something unpleasant clouds Kello's face.

KELLO

Citizens' committees! I didn't mean to hit the boy that hard. Yeah, that's when a feller needed a friend and I won't forget his initials, J. J.

The policeman in the car sticks his head out of the window.

PHIL
(to Hunsecker)

She died twenty minutes ago, Mr Hunsecker. They're still investigating.

55

HUNSECKER
(*shaking his head with total dismissal*)
That's show business. Thanks, Phil.
(*to Kello*)
See you.

ANOTHER ANGLE – 52ND STREET – NIGHT (DUSK)

Kello gets into the police car.

KELLO
(*as he does so*)
Hasta la vista, J. J. Hasta luego.

ANOTHER ANGLE. EXT. STREET – NIGHT

The car moves off eastward. Sidney and Hunsecker walk westward. Sidney, falling into step with Hunsecker, glances back at the departing police car.

SIDNEY
Spanish . . . that must show he likes 'spigs', too.

HUNSECKER
I like Harry, but I can't deny he sweats a little.

Camera now shoots down 52nd Street. Hunsecker, back to camera, studies the evening, hearing the sound of a screech of female laughter from one of the groups in the distance. A drunk is being thrown out of one of the strip-tease joints.

I love this dirty town.

Amused, Hunsecker turns back; he signals across the street to the car park, indicating that the big black Lincoln Continental should follow as he strolls with Sidney.

HUNSECKER – SIDNEY FOLLOWING

HUNSECKER
(*after a pause*)
Conjugate me a verb, Sidney. For instance, *to promise!*

Camera tracks with them in a close two shot. Sidney is alert now.

56

(*continuing*)
You told me you'd break up that romance – when?

SIDNEY
(*hesitantly*)
You want something done, J. J., but I doubt if you yourself
know what's involved.

HUNSECKER
(*soft and sardonic*)
I'm a schoolboy – teach me, teach me.

SIDNEY
(*carefully*)
Why not break it up yourself? You could do it in two minutes
flat.

Hunsecker pauses, halts.

HUNSECKER
(*harshly*)
At this late date you need explanations . . .? Susie's all I got –
now that she's growing up, I want my relationship with her to
stay at least at par! I don't intend to antagonize her if I don't
have to.
(*starting to walk again*)
Now, be warned, son – I'll have to blitz you . . .

Sidney follows quickly.

SIDNEY
Frankly, J. J., I don't think you got the cards to blitz me.

HUNSECKER
I don't?

SIDNEY
Correct me if I'm wrong, but I don't think so . . .

HUNSECKER
(*turning to eye him*)
I'll listen one more minute.

Sidney steps in front of Hunsecker, blocking his way for a moment.

57

SIDNEY
(*very rapidly*)

About a year ago, you asked me to do a favor. It was a thing –
well, I never did a thing that dirty in *all my life*.

*Hunsecker, totally disinterested in Sidney's problems of conscience,
signals to his car again, walks past Sidney, who continues rapidly:*

Awright, that brings us to five weeks ago. 'Sidney, I got a
nasty little problem here.' Did I say no? I'm frank to admit –
it don't jell as fast as we like . . . But all of a sudden *I can't get
you on the phone no more! Why?* . . . And why, as of this date,
am I frozen out of the column . . .

HUNSECKER
(*scornfully*)

Are you finished?

SIDNEY
(*quickly*)

No, lemme finish. *I don't like this job!* That boy is dumb only
on matinée days – otherwise he's got a head. And Susan, like
you said, she's growing up. Two heads. What I mean, we got
a slippery, dangerous problem here!

HUNSECKER
(*incisively*)

Not 'we', Sidney, you!

SIDNEY
(*gamely*)

Correct me if I'm wrong – *We!* Because when I'm out on
this very slippery limb for you, *you* have to know what's
involved.

HUNSECKER
(*sardonically*)

Ha! My right hand hasn't seen my left hand for thirty years!

Sidney quickly moves into J. J.'s path, desperate to hold his attention.

SIDNEY

I'll do it, J. J. – don't get me wrong – in for a penny, in for a pound. I'll see it through, but stop beating me around the head. *Let me make a living!*

> HUNSECKER
> (*his mouth tight and mean*)

What you promised – *do it!* Don't finagle around. It's later than you think.

Hunsecker walks past Sidney, now making for the car at which the attendant still waits.

> SIDNEY
> (*as Hunsecker passes him*)

Excuse it, but it's later than *you* think. That boy proposed tonight.

> HUNSECKER

Hunsecker is hit: he stops in his stride; he pauses and he turns slowly to look at Sidney. Lowering, he hesitates, mind clicking . . .

> HUNSECKER

Susie told you that . . .?

> REVERSE ANGLE FAVORING SIDNEY

Sidney, his eyes bright, nods. Hunsecker studies Sidney, then:

> HUNSECKER

No wonder you've been so 'feisty' tonight.

A pause.

> (*quietly*)

Can you deliver?

Sidney nods.

> SIDNEY

Uh huh.

> HUNSECKER

When?

SIDNEY

Tonight. Before you go to bed. The cat is in the bag and the bag is in the river.

HUNSECKER

Expressionless, he examines Sidney. Then he walks off toward the car. He tips the attendant, who thanks him, but instead of getting into the back of the car, he makes a small authoritative gesture to Nikko (double) to move over so that Hunsecker himself may drive. While Nikko does so, Hunsecker turns back to Sidney, whom the camera now includes.

HUNSECKER
(*quietly*)

Don't be a two-time loser, Sidalee. The sentence could be severe . . .

SIDNEY

He is satisfied.

HUNSECKER

Hunsecker gets into the driver's seat beside Nikko, the Japanese houseboy. Camera is close on Hunsecker who does not look back but is clearly aware of the position of Sidney as he puts the car into gear, revving the engine . . .

SIDNEY – NIGHT (DUSK)

The big car accelerates with impressive power. In doing so, it sends a cloud of fumes and a swirl of dust in Sidney's direction. He leaps out of the way, too late. Camera moves closer to him as, with anger and ignominy he inspects his precious clothing for damage. But, as he looks after the car, his face hardens into grim humor; he senses that this petty gesture from Hunsecker is an indication of his vulnerability, not his strength. As, dusting his coat, Sidney walks away, camera rises, watching his jaunty figure cross the street in the direction of 51st Street.

QUICK LAP DISSOLVE TO:

INT. TOOTS SHOR'S RESTAURANT – NIGHT

A long shot looking over the round bar toward the entrance. Sidney comes in through the revolving doors and comes toward camera. His eyes search among the crowd.

CLOSER ANGLE

REVERSE ANGLE

A Captain approaches Sidney.

> CAPTAIN
> Hello, Sidney, Wanna table?

> SIDNEY
> (*shaking his head*)
> Just hopping tonight. Leo Bartha been in?

> CAPTAIN
> Yeah, having supper with the missis. She's over there.

The Captain nods toward a booth on the other side of the bar where Mrs Bartha is sitting alone. Seeing that Bartha is not with her, the Captain looks around the bar . . .

> He's somewhere . . .

> SIDNEY
> (*interrupting*)
> Thanks, I see him . . .

Sidney is looking back toward the entrance hall, where . . .

BARTHA

Bartha comes forward (from the Men's Room) passing the Captain and Sidney. Sidney moves to intercept him.

> SIDNEY
> Hello, Leo. How goes that Sunday piece on cigarette girls?

ANOTHER ANGLE

A close shot on Bartha as he turns towards Sidney, stopping.

> BARTHA
> (*cautiously*)
> Who told you about it?

SIDNEY

Sidney smiles at Bartha, but the threat is clear.

> SIDNEY
> The cigarette girl . . . Rita. And she took out all her hairpins, too.

RESUME BARTHA

He throws a quick glance at his wife in the booth in background. Camera pulls back as Sidney, who has noted the look, moves closer to Bartha.

> SIDNEY
> I never had the pleasure of meeting your wife. You know what I wonder, Leo? Could you use a hot little item for tomorrow's column?

Sidney is pulling out of his pocket a pad on which to scribble the item. But Bartha faces him squarely, speaking sotto voce *but with emphasis.*

> BARTHA
> What is this, blackmail? Beat it!

Bartha turns on his heel and turns to walk toward his wife beyond.

SIDNEY

Sidney's face tightens. After a pause, he makes a decision and walks toward the booth.

BARTHA AND HIS WIFE

Bartha's wife is reading a tabloid and sipping champagne while her husband resumes eating a sandwich. These two are antagonists in a long war. Sidney comes up to the table, repeats:

SIDNEY

Leo, I've never had the pleasure of meeting your wife . . .

Bartha looks up. What can he do? Begrudgingly:

BARTHA

Loretta . . . Sidney Falco . . .

WIFE
(chatty)

How do you do, Mr Falco. If you know anything about
horses, sit a minute. Help yourself to a glass of this NY State
champagne – that's what my husband buys *me.*

*Mrs Bartha pushes the champagne bottle in Sidney's direction as Sidney
sits pleasantly; Bartha concentrates on his sandwich.*

SIDNEY

All the imported wines aren't what they're cracked up to be.

WIFE

Whose side are you on, Mr Falco, his or mine?

SIDNEY

Frankly, Mrs Bartha, I'm a neutral observer for the United
Nations.

WIFE

Mrs Bartha laughs, enjoying his deftness; then:

WIFE

What's your first name?

SIDNEY
(over scene)

Sidney.

*Mrs Bartha turns to concentrate on the names in the racing column of
the tabloid.*

63

WIFE
(*searching the column*)
No horse running tomorrow by that name . . .

BARTHA, WIFE AND SIDNEY

*An angle favoring Bartha and Sidney. Bartha glowers at his wife,
resenting the fact that she has permitted Sidney to join them.*

BARTHA
You ought to stop this nonsense, Loretta, these two-dollar
bets.

WIFE
(*cheerfully*)
It's compensation, Leo, for the marginal life we lead.
(*to Sidney*)
Sidney, did you hear the story about the cloak-and-suiter
who –?

BARTHA
(*sharply interrupting*)
That's right! Tell him, so I can read it in Hunsecker's column
first!

WIFE
(*to Sidney, brightly*)
Oh, are you a spy for the other side?

SIDNEY
No, I actually sat down to give Leo an item.

Sidney produces his pad again, begins to write on it.

WIFE
Leo, he wants to give you an item – don't be sullen.

Bartha notes Sidney's writing.

BARTHA
(*to his wife*)
Will you mind your own business!

                              WIFE
                            (calmly)
       Hitler!

She returns to her paper, ignoring them. Sidney finishes scribbling the
item.

                             SIDNEY
       Just in case you'd like to print it, Leo. It's a blind – no names
       mentioned. But for your private information, the guy's name
       is Dallas.

He pushes the item to Bartha, who reads it, briefly. Meanwhile:

                              WIFE
                  (concentrating on the tabloid)
       There isn't a single name here that gives off vibrations . . .

Bartha pushes the item back towards Sidney. Sidney glances quickly at
Bartha's stoney face then, significantly, turns toward his wife.

                             SIDNEY
       Anything there with a name like 'cigarette girl'?

Bartha raises his head, looks squarely at Sidney with contempt and
anger. His wife is unaware of this reaction. Still looking at the paper,
she murmurs:

                              WIFE
       Mmmmmm . . . 'cigarette girl' . . . No, no horse with a name
       like that . . .

Sidney pushes the item back towards Bartha.

       WIFE

Mrs Bartha's attention is attracted by Sidney's gesture. She looks up,
made aware of this strange by-play.

       BARTHA AND SIDNEY

A close two shot. Sidney waits; Bartha is white-lipped, but pushes the
item back again.

BARTHA

I don't print blind items.

RESUME WIFE

She looks from Sidney to her husband and back.

WIFE

What is this, chess or checkers . . .?

RESUME BARTHA, MRS BARTHA AND SIDNEY

A three shot favoring Bartha and Sidney. Both Sidney and Bartha are now aware of Mrs Bartha's curiosity.

SIDNEY
(*pointedly*)

Neither does Hunsecker.
(*fractional pause*)
He likes to use the real names . . .

A moment of chill silence. Then Bartha gets to his feet, signals for a waiter. As Sidney rises also:

WIFE

Where are we running? What am I missing here?

BARTHA

Waiter, the check.
(*to wife*)
This man is trying to hold a gun to my head!

WIFE
(*abruptly*)

That's the horse! Shotgun – Shotgun in the fifth!

She quickly studies her newspaper again. As quickly, Bartha leans across the table and snatches it out of her hands. In doing so, he upsets the glass of champagne, which contains only a few drops.

SIDNEY AND BARTHA

Bartha turns challengingly to Sidney.

BARTHA
(*sternly*)
What do you want to tell my wife, Sidney . . .?

WIFE

She is brushing her lap with her napkin.

WIFE
(*indignantly*)
He wants to tell me that you poured champagne all over my
lap.

RESUME BARTHA AND SIDNEY

Bartha ignores her, again challenges Sidney.

BARTHA
Go on, tell her, I'm waiting!

SIDNEY
(*flustered*)
What are you talking about? Are you nuts or what?

*The Waiter arrives in picture beside them, puts the check on the table
and goes. Bartha picks it up.*

RESUME WIFE

*Still mopping her dress with her napkin, she waits for her husband to
speak.*

BARTHA

He glances unhappily at his wife.

BARTHA
Lorry, I can't let this man blackmail me . . .

MRS BARTHA, BARTHA AND SIDNEY

*A three shot favoring Mrs Bartha, her husband and Sidney in
foreground.*

67

                              WIFE
    Blackmail . . .?

*Sidney decides to retreat. He turns, starts to go. But Bartha blocks his
way, holding Sidney and explaining to the Wife.*

                             BARTHA
    He wants me to print a dirty smear item for keeping his
    mouth shut.

A momentary pause. Then:
                              WIFE
    About what?

RESUME BARTHA

He is uneasy, ashamed of himself.

                             BARTHA
    Foolishly, Lorry, and I hope you'll understand . . . this
    cigarette girl . . . I was kidding around with her . . . this girl, I
    mean . . . I was kidding around and she took it seriously. It
    was a case of bad judgment, Lorry, bad taste . . . and I'm just
    sorry, Lorry, that's all . . .

RESUME WIFE

She says nothing.

RESUME BARTHA, SIDNEY AND MRS BARTHA

*The angle favoring Bartha and Sidney, Mrs Bartha in foreground.
Bartha now turns on Sidney.*

                             BARTHA
    Your friend Hunsecker – you can tell him for me – he's a
    disgrace to his profession. Never mind my bilious private life
    – I print a decent, responsible column – that's the way it
    stays! Your man – there's nothing he won't print if it satisfies
    his vanity or his spite! He'll use any spice to pepper up his
    daily garbage! Tell him I said so and that, like yourself, he's
    got the morals of a guinea pig and the scruples of a gangster!

                               68

Sidney tries to brazen it out, sneering:

SIDNEY

What do I do now? Whistle 'The Stars and Stripes Forever'?

Mrs Bartha slides along the seat, reaching for her fur.

MRS BARTHA

Camera pulls back with her as she collects her belongings, slides out between the tables and comes forward, passing Sidney to her husband.

WIFE
(*lightly*)

What you do now, Mr Falco, is crow like a hen – you have just laid an egg.

She presents her fur to her husband, and turns her back, inviting him to put it around her shoulders.

BARTHA AND WIFE

Another angle, favoring Bartha. He has not fully understood the significance of his wife's gesture. He studies her. She confirms his hopes as she adds:

                    WIFE
Leo, this is one of the cleanest things I've seen you do in
years . . .

With the fur around her shoulders, she turns and takes her husband's arm with some pride. They walk away. Camera eases back to include Sidney. He is angry at himself – more for the failure of his efforts at blackmail than any sense of shame at the attempt.

OTIS ELWELL

A medium long shot. At a booth on the other side of the bar sits a dapper gentleman with a twinkle of malice in his eyes. He has been watching the altercation with keen interest and satisfaction. Elwell gives some instructions to a waiter who is serving him with drinks, pointing toward Sidney.

    SIDNEY

Sidney's face shows a burning resentment. He glances about him to see how much of the embarrassing scene has been observed. As he moves away, the Waiter walks into shot, addressing him.

WAITER

The Waiter approaches Sidney. He has a message.

                  WAITER
Otis Elwell wants to see you, Sidney.

The Waiter nods toward the other side of the circular bar. Sidney, his humiliation and rage still burning, looks off toward . . .

OTIS ELWELL

From Sidney's viewpoint. Elwell beckons.

SIDNEY

*He comes round the circular bar. He shows no eagerness to join Elwell,
but approaches the table. Elwell makes a gesture, inviting Sidney to sit.
Sidney doesn't accept it.*

ELWELL
(*pleasantly*)
I see Bartha gave you cold tongue for supper.
(*as Sidney starts to leave*)
Hey, wait a minute!

SIDNEY
(*hesitating*)
I'm late for a date with a dame.

*Then, returning, he leans over the table addressing Elwell with quiet
anger.*

Otis, if you're trying to blow this brawl into an item for your
column – *forget it!*

REVERSE ANGLE

*Across Sidney and Elwell. Elwell is quietly enjoying Sidney's display of
hurt dignity.*

ELWELL
(*affably*)
How is dear old J. J. by the way?

SIDNEY
(*his anger relapsing*)
Call him up and ask – he might drop dead with shock.

ELWELL
(*lightly*)
If it were that easy, you wouldn't find an empty phone booth
for the next two hours . . .

SIDNEY

*A close shot. While Elwell continues, he is not looking at Sidney.
Elwell's expression of dislike of Hunsecker is not over-emphatic; but*

71

Sidney senses, nevertheless, that it is very real – and this gives him a new idea.

> ELWELL
> (*continuing over scene*)
> . . . Talk of a wake! They'd club each other to cater the affair for free!

RESUME ELWELL AND SIDNEY

Elwell looks up at Sidney as he continues.

> ELWELL
> (*happily*)
> By the way, did I hear something about J. J. giving you the flit gun treatment – he shut you out of the column.
> (*amused*)
> Why?

REVERSE ANGLE

Sidney has rapidly resumed his manner of resentment (in order to exploit Elwell's dislike of Hunsecker).

> SIDNEY
> You don't know that lunatic yet? Whims – egotistic whims! Like the gag – when you got him for a friend, you don't need an enemy!
> (*a pause, then:*)
> That's what the fight with Bartha was about. 'Leo,' I says, 'Hunsecker froze me out. So I'm eating humble pie this month – please print me an item.'

> ELWELL
> (*pleased*)
> And, instead, he printed his heel in your face?

> SIDNEY
> (*morose*)
> I see you're full of human feelings . . .

72

ELWELL

He has lost interest in Sidney.

ELWELL
(*with a shrug*)
Like most of the human race, Sidney, I'm bored. I'd go a
mile for a chuckle . . .

Elwell's voice fades: his attention has been caught by . . .

REVERSE ANGLE

*. . . three people are passing the table, squeezing their way past; a man
with two very fetching young women. Elwell's eyes are riveted to the
anatomy that is temptingly displayed.*

SIDNEY
(*noting Elwell's pre-occupation*)
. . . and two miles for a pretty girl . . .?

ELWELL

He is unembarrassed at Sidney's all-too-accurate estimate.

ELWELL
(*lightly*)
Three . . . even four . . .

*Elwell turns back toward the papers on his table, a zippered document
case and some publications among which a columnist might search for
scandal; among these is a magazine of semi-pornographic nature.*

(*continuing, casually*)
Then you're really washed up with Hunsecker . . .?

REVERSE ANGLE

*The nature of Elwell's reading tastes is also not lost on Sidney. With his
eyes glancing at the magazine, Sidney now accepts the original offer to
sit down. He produces the slip of paper that Bartha rejected, offering it
as illustration.*

SIDNEY

This is how much I'm washed with J. J . . .

As Elwell reads, Sidney continues giving a passing scrutiny – apparently casual – to a picture of a girl on the magazine cover.

Look, Otis, I make no brief for my bilious private life, but he's got the morals of a guinea pig and the scruples of a gangster.

Elwell shows no undue enthusiasm for the item.

ELWELL
(*drily*)

A fine, fat dirty item.
(*offering it back to Sidney*)
Who's it about?

But Sidney doesn't take the paper back; he explains:

SIDNEY

A kid named Dallas, who runs a dinky jazz quintet.
(*he leans closer*)
He keeps company with J. J.'s screwball sister . . .

ELWELL

This does get a reaction, a flicker of genuine interest. Elwell reads the item for a second time.

SIDNEY AND ELWELL

Watching Elwell read, Sidney encourages:

SIDNEY

It's a real goody if, like me, you wanna clobber J. J.!

Now Elwell lays the item down in front of him. Clearly, he is considering it. Sidney prompts again.

He's got his TV tomorrow. He'd read it just before rehearsals.

Elwell nods. But he is still reluctant.

74

ELWELL
(*cautiously*)
Mmm. Trouble is I can't think of any good reason why I
should print anything you give me. I can't even think of a *bad*
reason.

SIDNEY

*Sidney drops his eyes to the magazine once more. He fingers it in a
preoccupied but significant way.*

SIDNEY
(*gently*)
Suppose I introduce you to a *lovely* reason, Otis. One that's
good *and* bad . . . and available?

ELWELL

His eyes go from the magazine to Sidney; he gets the point alright.

ELWELL
I'm not an unreasonable man . . .

Elwell reaches for the slip of paper once more.

SIDNEY AND ELWELL

*In picking it up, Elwell clearly implies his readiness to accept the item –
on conditions. Sidney, in his turn, gets* this *point. He turns toward the
passing waiter.*

SIDNEY
Waiter! The check.

LAP DISSOLVE TO:

INT. SIDNEY'S APARTMENT – NIGHT

*Rita is in the bedroom. She appears to have some familiarity with the
premises . . . She hears the doorbell. She makes swift adjustment to her
appearance and takes a swift gulp of a drink as she carries it through to
answer the door.*

75

SIDNEY'S OFFICE

The outer room is lit only by one of the lamps on the desk. Rita crosses and goes to the door. Sidney's shadow can be seen through the frosted glass. At the door, Rita opens it slowly and with a seductive manner.

> RITA
> *(coyly)*

Hi!

Sidney steps into the room. Rita begins to close the door prior to stepping into his embrace. Sidney puts one arm about her. But now she reacts to . . .

ANOTHER ANGLE

Otis Elwell stands on the landing outside. In most gentlemanly fashion, he takes off his hat.

RITA

This new arrival gets a dismal reaction from the girl.

> SIDNEY
> *(unembarrassed)*

Rita, say hello to Otis Elwell.

> RITA
> *(with no welcome whatsoever)*

Hello.

ANOTHER ANGLE

Elwell is not unaware of his cool reception. He glances at Sidney as he comes into the room. But his manner is suave.

> ELWELL

Friends call me Otis – sometimes Tricky Otis.

> SIDNEY

Otis was outraged when I told him Van Cleve was going to fire you.

RITA
(*blankly*)

He was . . .?

Elwell now gets a good look at Rita; his brow wrinkles.

ELWELL
(*to Rita*)

Don't I know you from somewhere? Saratoga? Last
summer . . .?

RITA

*She knows something, but says nothing. She shakes her head. Sidney
seems eager to ease the tension in the room.*

SIDNEY
(*soothingly to Rita*)

Relax. Take some weight off those lovely gams. Let me fix
your drink.

ELWELL
(*following Sidney's lead*)

Rita, when you look at me, you look at a friend in disguise.
(*another wrinkling of the brow*)

Miami Beach two years ago . . .?

RITA

Haven't been in Florida since I was a little girl . . .

ELWELL
(*accepting a drink from Sidney*)

Well, here's to the time we played with dolls, but dreamed of
better things . . .
(*exploring the room*)

Cozy place you've got here, snug.

Rita has left open the door into the bedroom. Elwell looks through it.

SIDNEY

Make yourself at home.
(*to Rita*)

Otis carries a lot of weight with your boss, honey. He's going to

tell him not to pay any attention to anything you-know-who says about you-know-what.
>   (*to Otis*)
Right, Otis?

>   ELWELL
Right!

Elwell sits down on the settee, stretches his limbs, smiles at the girl. Rita still says nothing. Sidney mistakes her attitude for acquiescence. He swallows his drink, sets it down.

>   SIDNEY
I thought you two could talk the whole thing over till I got back.

Rita looks at him sharply.

>   RITA
Back?

>   SIDNEY
One of those business meetings, honey – always coming up in the middle of the night.

He grins at Rita. She doesn't respond. Turning, she goes swiftly through the door into the bedroom.

>   RITA
>   (*sharply*)
Hold on. You can drop me off on your way . . .

Emphasizing the asperity in her voice, she closes the door behind her.

ANOTHER ANGLE

Elwell looks at Sidney; Sidney looks at Elwell. Elwell gets up slowly from the settee.

>   ELWELL
>   (*amused by acid*)
Consternation reigns . . .

Sidney is uncomfortable, not sure how Elwell is taking the rejection. Elwell glances at his wristwatch, lays down his drink.

SIDNEY
(*quickly*)

Now, Otis . . .

Elwell shrugs, remarks pleasantly but with significance:

ELWELL

I hate J. J. – but not that much at this moment . . .

SIDNEY

Give me a chance –

He goes into the bedroom, closing the door after him.

INT. BEDROOM

Rita is in a flurry of indignation. Sitting on the bed, she is fastening one high-heeled shoe. Sidney stands glaring at her.

SIDNEY

Don't you know who that man is?

RITA
(*bitingly*)

Yeah. Otis Elwell. The columnist.

SIDNEY
(*nodding with emphasis*)

Yeah!

RITA
(*aggressively*)

And he's a perfect stranger to me.

SIDNEY
(*explosively*)

So take five minutes! Get acquainted! He's an important man
– he's lonely – don't be dumb!

Rita, with one shoe on, has begun to search for the other.

RITA

What do you want all of a sudden – Lady Godiva . . .?
Where's my other shoe?

SIDNEY

What kind of an act is this?

Rita jumps to her feet. Her righteous indignation is handicapped by the lop-sided stance caused by the lack of one shoe.

RITA

Don't you think I have any feelings? What am I? A bowl of fruit? A tangerine that peels in a minute?

SIDNEY

(*caustic*)

I beg your pardon! I turn myself inside out to help you and now I'm a heavy.

(*stooping swiftly as he discovers her shoe*)

Here's your shoe, there's your coat, that's the door!

Contemptuously he thrusts the coat and the shoe into her arms. The positive force of his manner gives the girl pause. There is a silence. Rita searches for words to explain the offense to her sensibilities.

RITA

Sidney . . . I . . . I don't do this sort of thing . . .

SIDNEY

What sort of thing?

RITA
(*emphatic*)

This sort of thing!

SIDNEY
(*as emphatic*)

Listen, you need him for a favor, don't you! And so do I!
I need his column – *tonight.*
(*then*)
Didn't you ask me to do something about your job? Don't
you have a kid in Military School?

A pause. Sidney has struck brutally home. Rita's lower lip trembles.

RITA

You're a snake, Falco. You're a louse, a real louse.

*Sidney's manner becomes swiftly sympathetic – but still urgent. He turns
to the door and picks up the glasses she has set down on the table behind
it.*

SIDNEY
(*as he opens the door*)

How many snorts does it take to put you in that Tropical
Island Mood?

Sidney goes out.

SIDNEY'S OFFICE

*Elwell overhears the last remark and as Sidney passes him, he winks.
While Sidney pours another drink, Elwell faces the doorway. Rita comes
into it, stands on the threshold. She is still far from enthusiastic.*

ELWELL
(*an inspiration*)

Havana! That's where we met!

Rita shakes her head morosely. Sidney comes and puts a stiff drink into her hand. Elwell raises the glass, toasting the girl, encouraging her to drink. Rita responds dimly.

>   RITA
>   (*to Otis*)
> Here's mud in your column!

Sidney laughs, more from relief than from the joke.

>   SIDNEY
> Blessings on thee, the both . . . well . . . Gotta run now. See you two kids later!

>   ELWELL
>   (*lightly*)
> Hurry back.

At the door Sidney takes cheerful leave of them.

>   SIDNEY
> Don't do anything I wouldn't do. That gives you lots of leeway.

HALLWAY OUTSIDE SIDNEY'S APARTMENT

Closing the door, Sidney seems pleased with himself. He goes swiftly down the stairs.

INT. SIDNEY'S OFFICE

Rita remains on the threshold of the doorway between the two rooms. There is an uncomfortable silence. Elwell carries it off by coming to the girl, offering her a cigarette. She accepts it. Elwell studies her, smiling affectionately. Rita meets his eyes, avoids them again, then quietly offers the information:

>   RITA
> Palm Springs. Two years ago.

Elwell begins to laugh. Whatever the memory, it seems to amuse him vastly because he continues to laugh.

ELWELL
(*delighted*)

That's right!

Rita drinks. She adds glumly:

RITA

Don't tell Sidney.

Elwell continues to laugh as we . . .

CUT TO:

ORANGE JUICE STAND – NIGHT

Shooting east on 46th Street walks Sidney, coming out of the entrance of his apartment, toward camera. He is pleased with himself, satisfied with his ingenuity in dealing with Rita and Bartha.

The streets behind him are dark and empty (it is about three in the morning). Camera moves with Sidney as he steps briskly into the orange juice stand and lifts the receiver from the pay telephone. There are no other customers at the counter, but the man behind is squeezing orange halves for the day ahead, piling up a mountain of empties some of which fall at Sidney's feet.

EXT. HUNSECKER'S PENTHOUSE

Camera shoots up at the penthouse on the roof of the Brill Building. The Budweiser sign is extinguished, a black silhouette against the sky. A light burns in the window of Hunsecker's apartment. (This is painted in the matte shot.)

INT. HUNSECKER'S APARTMENT – NIGHT

The ringing of the telephone is heard in the big room – an impressively furnished apartment which has a decor indicating that the owner thinks of himself in epic terms.

Camera moves to discover Hunsecker in robe and pajamas, tapping at his typewriter. Taking his leisurely time, he picks up the phone and eventually answers it.

83

HUNSECKER
(*to phone*)
Yes . . . ? You sound happy, Sidney. Why should you be
happy when I'm not?
(*then*)
I'll see the papers when I get up. How do you spell Picasso,
the French painter?

*He languidly writes down Picasso on his scratch pad, answering a
query, drily.*

It's an item – I hear he goes out with three-eyed girls.

RESUME ORANGE JUICE STAND – NIGHT

*Camera shoots past Sidney at the phone toward Broadway, which is
now deserted. A street-flushing truck goes by, moving through the dead
city.*

SIDNEY
(*to phone*)
It would be nice if you mentioned R-O-B-A-R-D – Robard's
jazz joint – it's his twentieth anniversary. Don't begrudge it to
me, J. J. – I owe him lots of favors.
(*glancing toward the attendant to see that he has not overheard*)
I think you understand, don't you, that the Dallas skull is
badly dented? Oh, real bad . . . starting today, you can play
marbles with his eyeballs.
(*even coquetting*)
Don't hold out on me, J. J., mention Robard.

RESUME HUNSECKER'S APARTMENT – NIGHT

*Hunsecker is writing Robard's name on his pad, but he says into the
phone:*

HUNSECKER
We shall see what we shall see . . .
(*lazily*)
And don't ever use this apartment phone again; I have a
nervous sister.

He cradles the phone, looks at it for a moment, switches his eyes and then physically follows them, rising to stroll toward the glass doors onto the terrace. He moves out and turns aside to look in at the adjoining window, which belongs to Susan's bedroom.

INT. SUSAN'S BEDROOM – NIGHT

Camera shoots across Susan in foreground; she is asleep, a tired, helpless, sweet kid. The figure of her brother is seen – a dark shape on the terrace outside. He moves away across the terrace.

EXT. TERRACE – NIGHT

Hunsecker turns from the window. Camera is close on his brooding face. Camera tracks with him as he crosses toward the parapet. At this height there is a wind which blows his hair and the movement of the camera emphasizes a remarkable vista of the New York skyline. The buildings are now dark, only a few of the electric signs are left on all night. Camera comes to rest looking over Hunsecker's shoulder; it tilts downward to a view of Broadway below, Duffy Square in the distance.

HUNSECKER

A close up; Hunsecker is looking down on his 'kingdom'. But there is little love in the man's face, only authoritarian power.

EXT. FROM THE TERRACE – NIGHT

From Hunsecker's viewpoint. The streets empty, except for an occasional passing taxi. The street-flushing truck comes up Broadway from Duffy Square . . .

LAP DISSOLVE THROUGH TO:

EXT. FROM THE TERRACE – DAY

The identical camera set-up. Through the dissolve the light changes from night to day; Broadway magically becomes a roaring stream of traffic.

EXT. GLOBE BUILDING – DAY

In foreground a News Vendor. Sidney comes out of the exit of a subway, reaching for his pocket as he approaches the News Vendor who offers him a paper.

> NEWS VENDOR

The Globe?

> SIDNEY
> (*shaking his head*)

Gimme *The Record.*

Sidney buys and opens the paper. Camera moves closer to shoot over his shoulder. We see the gossip column which bears a photograph of Otis Elwell at the top. Smirking with satisfaction, Sidney turns away from the camera and throws the paper into a trash basket before he disappears into the impressive entrance of a large office building. The sign above the doorway reads: THE NEW YORK GLOBE.

QUICK DISSOLVE TO:

INT. GLOBE BUILDING – DAY

Mary, Hunsecker's secretary, occupies a cubicle which is separated from the rest of the newsroom by a partition. From the big room beyond comes the hum and chatter of much activity, typewriters and the urgent murmur of the staff of a big newspaper. The walls of Mary's cubicle are covered with photographs; filing cabinets are piled high with unopened mail; two wire service teletype machines click desultorily. Mary is plain but attractive, past thirty, a level-headed woman with a sense of integrity. She is on the phone just now, bored with the insistent voice on the other end. Beside her an earnest young Lawyer waits with several papers in hand.

> MARY
> (*to phone*)

I have no power to retract, Mr Cummings . . . I'm only Mr Hunsecker's secretary. No. Nor can I agree that any retraction is necessary. Thank you for calling.

Sidney has come through the newsroom in background. He pauses tactfully, seeing Mary occupied with the Lawyer.

LAWYER
(*huffily*)
I fail to see what's amusing about these papers.

MARY
I'll get the boss to sign them.

LAWYER
(*giving her the papers*)
They're important.

MARY
You've said that six times – that's why I'm smiling.

As the disgruntled Lawyer leaves, Sidney comes in, wearing his most winning smile. With a glance after the Lawyer, making sure that he is not observed, Sidney greets Mary, assuming a brogue:

SIDNEY
Hello, Mary, me darlin' and phwat are ye up to today?

Sidney's hand caresses her shoulder with a gesture which indicates a certain intimacy between them.

MARY
That's a question I usually like to ask *you*. Your secretary phoned.

SIDNEY
What about?

MARY
(*shrugging*)
Something about a Frank D'Angelo trying to reach you . . .

Sidney reaches for the phone. As he does so, Mary hesitates and glances at a copy of The Record *which lies on the desk open at Otis Elwell's column. She picks it up.*

MARY
(*continuing*)
Is that the man who manages Susie's boyfriend?

Sidney murmurs casually, 'Yeah. Why?' as he dials. Mary holds up the paper, indicating the item.

Have you seen this? In Otis Elwell's column.
                              (*reads*)
'The dreamy marijuana smoke of a lad who heads a
highbrow jazz quintet is giving an inelegant odor to that
elegant East Side club where he works. That's no way for a
card-holding Party Member to act. Moscow won't like, you
naughty boy!'

*Sidney accepts the paper from Mary, examines the item while he talks to
Sally on the phone.*

                         SIDNEY
                      (*into phone*)
Sally? I got the message. If D'Angelo calls again, tell him I'll
be at the office around noon.

He hangs up, continuing to read.

                          MARY
Could this be that boy?

SIDNEY
(*casually*)
Dallas? Could be. He doesn't look like a reefer smoker . . .

He discards the paper with a show of disinterest. Mary picks it up again.

MARY
(*looking at* The Record *again*)
If this is true, J. J.'s going to hit the ceiling . . .

Sidney moves around behind Mary. His eyes are fixed on a spike which sits on Mary's desk. On it is impaled a proof of Hunsecker's column. Meanwhile, he remarks:

SIDNEY
Can it be news to you that J. J.'s ceiling needs a plaster job every six weeks?

INSERT

From Sidney's viewpoint, Hunsecker's column. The shot is just too distant for us to be able to read the print.

SIDNEY AND MARY

Sidney is looking at the column. Mary is concentrating on papers before her. Without looking up, she is clearly aware of Sidney's efforts to read the proof.

MARY
(*quietly*)
Sidney, you know that J. J. doesn't like people to look at the column proof in advance . . .

Sidney, caught 'in flagrante', laughs.

SIDNEY
Mary, I'm not 'people' – there's Falco blood, sweat and tears in that column.

He turns away, changing the subject (apparently).

SIDNEY

How about dinner tonight?

Mary turns to study him.

MARY

Bribing me again?

SIDNEY
(uncomfortable under her scrutiny)

And why should I bribe the woman who holds most of my heart?

Mary is thoughtful. Without malice, in a detached sort of way, she examines Sidney.

MARY

You're a real rascal, Sidney. I'd certainly dislike you if I didn't like you. You're an amusing boy, but there isn't a drop of respect in you for anything alive – you're too immersed in the theology of making a fast buck. Not that I don't sometimes feel that you yearn for something better . . .

Sidney finds this analysis hard to take. Again he tries to laugh his way out of it.

SIDNEY
(cynical)

Mary, don't try to sell me the Brooklyn Bridge. I happen to know it belongs to the Dodgers.

Mary, smiling, decides 'to let him off the hook'. She takes the spike and the column and passes it across to Sidney's side of the desk, as she returns briskly to her business.

MARY
(affably)

I don't mind you looking at the proof of the column in advance, as long as J. J. doesn't know. But don't do it like a boy stealing gum from a slot-machine.

Sidney doesn't like this; but, on the other hand, he does *want to look at the column. After only a momentary struggle, he picks the column off the spike and reads.*

SIDNEY
Who put this item in about the comic?
(*reading*)
'If there's a more hilarious funny man around than Herbie
Temple at the Palace, you'll have to pardon us for not
catching the name. We were too busy screaming.' Does this
Temple have a press agent?

MARY
No. It's one of J. J.'s occasional *beaux gestes*. Evidently the
fellow's funny, so he gave him a plug.

He goes to the door, grinning.

SIDNEY
What's your favorite ribbon to go around your favorite
chocolates?

MARY
Let's wait till Christmas – it's more legitimate then.

She looks after Sidney, thinks about him for a moment. Then she types.

EXT. PALACE THEATRE – DAY

*Sidney comes down 47th Street from Broadway, making for the stage
door entrance of the Palace Theatre. He walks confidently into the
alleyway, paying no attention to the old Doorman gossiping with the
shoeshine boy at the chairs next to the entrance. The Doorman turns,
protesting:*

DOORMAN
(*calling out*)
Hey!

LAP DISSOLVE TO:

*Sidney, without halting, looks back toward the Doorman, addressing
him with the patronizing manner of a superior.*

SIDNEY
Herbie Temple here yet?

DOORMAN
Yeah, but you can't come in now!

SIDNEY
I'm in, Sonny Boy!

He is already on his way into doorway.

INT. BACKSTAGE. PALACE THEATRE

The movie will soon be finished and the comedian who opens the stage show is ready and made-up in the wings. He sits with his agent, Al Evans, a small, worried, bespectacled man, who waves an unlighted cigar as big as himself. They converse in loud whispers, talking against the muffled and echoing sound of the film soundtrack, silhouetted against the ghostly, distorted images on the big screen seen at a weird angle behind them.

EVANS
I didn't waste words, Herbie, take my word. I says, 'Look, Figo, I'm not selling you a dozen eggs, I'm selling you Herbie Temple,' I says, 'so don't gimme your lip!'

The comedian, Herbie Temple, looks up. Sidney comes through a fireproof door which separates the stage from the corridors to dressing-rooms. In background two chorus girls in costume are squeezed into a telephone booth. Sidney joins the comedian and the agent; he smiles at the comedian, while he addresses the agent.

SIDNEY
Hiya, Al!

The agent looks from Sidney to Temple, surprised and displeased.

EVANS
Since when did you two get acquainted?

Sidney has clearly never met Temple; blandly he chooses to regard the agent's remark as an introduction; he offers his hand with generous amiability.

SIDNEY
How do you do, Mr Temple . . .

The comic accepts the hand doubtfully.

> TEMPLE
> (*uncertain*)

Delighted.

> SIDNEY

I'm Sidney Falco.

> TEMPLE
> (*still dubious*)

Yeah, delighted . . .

Evans stand up, warns the comic.

> EVANS

Watch this guy, Herbie, he's a press agent.

Temple's smile congeals.

> TEMPLE

You watch him, Al, I s . . . s . . . stutter!

> SIDNEY
> (*in no way discouraged*)

Temple, I caught your act the other night and –

> TEMPLE

Did you now? On which bounce?

> SIDNEY

– and I just had to drop by and tell you how great I thought
you were.

> TEMPLE
> (*drily*)

Cheers. What time is it, Al?

> EVANS

You got ten minutes.
> (*to Sidney*)

Hope you don't mind, Falco: we're busy and if –

Sidney stands up.

93

No, I don't mind. I'm busy too.

TEMPLE
(*scowling*)
Good! We're all off to Utica, so excuse us, Mr Frannis-on-the-Portisan.

Sidney moves toward the doorway onto the corridor. The chorus girls have now vacated the phone booth.

SIDNEY
But can I ask one impertinent question here? With no criticism intended, because I know, Al, you earn your ten percent, how come you let a sock act like Herbie Temple tiptoe through town without a publicity build . . .?

Smiling, wise, Evans shakes his head.

EVANS
We're not buying it, Falco – no fish today.

Sidney presses, as if annoyed.

SIDNEY
I'm not selling. I'm just curious, that's all.

Temple turns away from Sidney, leaving him to Evans.

TEMPLE
Answer the man, Al, if he asks you a question. Quick, before he thinks up another!

Evans moves to Sidney, trying to shepherd him out the way he came.

EVANS
Mr Temple doesn't believe in press agents – does that answer you something?

ANOTHER ANGLE

Evans makes the mistake of laying a hand on Sidney's elbow. Sidney doesn't like people touching him. He reacts in anger, as we have seen before – fixes a burning eye on Evans.

SIDNEY

Take your hand off, lump!
(*more politely to Temple*)
No one believes in press agents, Temple, when they make
claims they can't perform. I got nothing to sell – I didn't
come here to peddle – but if I tell a client that Hunsecker will
give him space, it's not just talk!

*Sidney steps briskly up the stairs into the corridor. Evans, angry, is
stalled for a moment of delayed action by mention of the magic name of
Hunsecker.*

EVANS
(*after hesitation*)
Listen, you bull-artist – !

TEMPLE

Let him go, Al . . .

SIDNEY

But Sidney has already stepped to the phone booth and is dialling.

95

> SIDNEY
> *(to phone)*
Hello? Mary, let me speak to J. J., please . . . it's Sidney
Falco . . .

REVERSE ANGLE

*Shooting past Sidney in foreground onto Temple and Evans beyond,
they watch him, open-mouthed. Sidney notes their reaction.*

> SIDNEY
> *(to phone)*
Tell him it's important . . .

INT. SIDNEY'S APARTMENT – DAY

Sally is at her desk, bewildered as she speaks into the phone.

> SALLY
What? Is this Sidney? . . .

RESUME BACKSTAGE. PALACE THEATRE – DAY

> SIDNEY
> *(to phone)*
Sure, I'll wait . . .

*While doing so, he glances back with disinterest at Evans and Temple.
The comedian and the agent exchange looks. Evans is uneasy; he comes
up the steps into the corridor to address Sidney with a deflated manner.*

> EVANS
> *(hesitant)*
Look, nobody hired you! We didn't talk any deal, and –

*With his hand over the mouthpiece, Sidney addresses Evans with
contempt.*

> SIDNEY
Relax, lump! I told you I'm not selling fish . . .
> *(abruptly reverting to the phone)*
J.J. . . . Sidney! . . . How are you, sweetheart?

(*laughing*)
Yeah . . .
(*then seriously*)
Listen, I know it's late, J. J., but is it too late to add
something important to the column?
(*grinning*)
No, not a relative, but important . . .

RESUME SALLY. INT. SIDNEY'S APARTMENT

*Shaking her head, Sally places the phone down on the desk, looks at it
as it chatters away. She considers returning to her typing, but, worried,
picks the phone up again. Sidney's chattering voice is barely audible:
'You know Herbie Temple, the comic . . .? What about him? He's at
the Palace and he's great. That's what about him. And you'd do me a
big bunny basket of a favor if you would say it in tomorrow's column.'*

RESUME BACKSTAGE. PALACE THEATRE

Temple and Evans are now staring at Sidney with considerable respect.

REVERSE ANGLE

*The comedian and the agent in foreground, Sidney still on the phone
beyond.*

SIDNEY
(*off-screen*)
Yeah, if you got a pencil there I'll suggest a word or two. Uh
. . . Uh . . .

*The comedian and the agent in foreground, Sidney still on the phone
beyond.*
(*to phone, continuing*)
If there's a funnier man in the world than Herbie Temple at
the Palace . . . uh . . . pardon us for not catching the name,
we were too busy laughing. No, make that 'screaming'.
(*then*)
It's sweet of you, J. J., thanks. Probably see you at Twenty-
One tonight. No, for supper, late. Right. Bye . . .

He hangs up.

97

TEMPLE

Speak to this lad, Al . . . to Mr Falco.

SIDNEY

See me in my office.

He turns and walks away down the corridor. As he vanishes, Temple starts after him.

Sidney walks off in the direction of the exit – (not so fast that he can't be overtaken). Temple hurries into the corridor and comes after him. Evans also follows, though not so eagerly.

TEMPLE

Wait a minute.
            (*turning back to encourage Evans*)
Speak to him, Al.
                  (*to Sidney, apologetically*)
Al makes all my deals.

Sidney permits himself to be detained.

SIDNEY
                  (*coolly, looking toward Evans*)
I don't like a guy that's quick with the hands.
                  (*to Temple*)
Temple, you've been three passes behind for twenty years.
This could start you off big – TV and anywhere.

Evans, not as wholly convinced as the comedian, comes up to join them. Temple looks at the agent.

TEMPLE

And it would cost a pretty penny, huh?

SIDNEY
                  (*to Evans*)
You tell him, I stutter!

EVANS
                  (*shrewdly*)
Uh . . . Why don't we wait till tomorrow?

Sidney, shrugging, makes a negligent exit.

SIDNEY
(*as he goes*)
Wait as long as you like – you know where my office is.

They look after him. Evans' face is cold and suspecting, but Temple's face contains fresh warmth.

DISSOLVE TO:

STAIRS OUTSIDE SIDNEY'S OFFICE – DAY

Sidney comes briskly up the stairs. Outside his door he pauses, listens, hearing the murmur of voices inside. Then he walks in casually.

INT. SIDNEY'S OFFICE – DAY

Sidney steps in, closing the door. He pretends surprise as he sees . . .

ANOTHER ANGLE

. . . Steve and D'Angelo waiting for him. Sidney comes into shot, Sally remains at her desk while Steve and D'Angelo are silent, looking at Sidney.

SIDNEY
(*perkily*)
What is here, a wake?

D'Angelo rises from the couch, crossing to Sidney to hand him a copy of the tabloid, The Record. *It is folded open at Elwell's column. As he passes it to Sidney, D'Angelo marks with his thumbnail an item near the bottom of the column. Sidney takes the paper and reads. (He reads a little too quickly.) Then he hands it back to D'Angelo.*

ANOTHER ANGLE

Steve notes Sidney's too perfunctory reading.

STEVE
You read as you run, don't you?

Sidney turns on Steve, coldly:

SIDNEY

It's a habit with me. So now I'm briefed. So what?

STEVE
(*glancing at D'Angelo*)
Frank thinks I shouldn't have come here –

D'ANGELO
(*a quick correction*)
Excuse me, Steve. I said namely you shouldn't go around wild, blaming people without justification.

STEVE
(*watchfully, to Sidney*)
I thought you might have a faint idea of how this item originated.

REVERSE ANGLE

Favoring Sidney. He pauses.

SIDNEY

Why me . . .?

STEVE

Why not you?

SIDNEY

That's your idea of logic? I tell the judge I didn't murder the man – the judge says, 'Why *not* you?'

STEVE

Only two men in this town could be responsible for that smear – you or Hunsecker or both.

SIDNEY
(*explosively*)
Dallas, ask your own manager – he's standing here like a pained wolfhound – *Hunsecker and Elwell are enemies to the knife.* So how do you get him doing J. J. a favor?

STEVE
(*quickly*)
It *is* a favor, isn't it?

SIDNEY
(*as quickly*)
According to you, yeah.
(*continuing rapidly and with heat*)
Dallas, your mouth is as big as a basket and twice as empty! I
don't like you, comma, but neither do I go along with this
column saying you smoke marijuana and belong with the
Reds. Also, since we're talking repulsive, J. J. won't like this
for two cents! Don't give me that look, Dallas – J. J. believes
in fair play. And secondly, this could splatter his sister with
rotten egg by implication – you're her boyfriend!

RESUME REVERSE ANGLE

*Sidney's manner is a little too vigorous. (In adopting an aggressive
tone, he is really trying to needle Steve.) Steve, though on the verge of
losing his temper, is sharp enough to notice the point.*

STEVE
You're talking very fast.

SIDNEY
(*expostulating*)
Well, I'll tell you what – excuse me for breathing, will ya?
(*wheeling to Sally*)
How do you like it? He comes to *my* office and –

D'ANGELO

Sensing the danger, D'Angelo moves forward soothingly between them.

D'ANGELO
Boys, this gets nobody nowhere – you're overexcited, Steve
and –

STEVE
(*sharply*)
Don't apologize for me, Frank!

D'ANGELO
. . . excited with good reason, I wanted to say.

(*to Sidney*)
Because this endangers the future of the whole quintet . . .

SIDNEY
(*lightly*)
Should I cry . . .?

Steve, with a glare at both men, goes to the phone on Sally's desk. He dials.

D'ANGELO
(*continuing*)
. . . People catch on quick to such an item. Van Cleve already called me – he's firing the quintet.

SIDNEY
Then what are you doing here? Go over there and fight! If Van Cleve fires your boy, it gives a lie the ring of truth!

In background Steve speaks quietly into the phone.

STEVE
I want to speak to Miss Hunsecker, please.

D'ANGELO
(*replying to Sidney's question*)
We're on our way there now . . .

SIDNEY
(*who has wheeled on Steve*)
What are you calling *her* for . . .?

STEVE

Sidney's reaction to the mention of Susan's name gives Steve food for thought. While he waits for Susan to be summoned to the phone, he studies Sidney.

STEVE
(*to Sidney*)
I'm the boyfriend, remember? I hope one day she'll be my wife . . .
(*into the phone, gently*)
This is Steve, Susie. Don't be alarmed, Susie, but I want you

to look at Elwell's column in *The Record*. . . today . . . No, about me . . .

INT. HUNSECKER'S APARTMENT. SUSAN'S BEDROOM – DAY

Susan is on the phone. Listening to what Steve says, she is frightened – almost too frightened; it is as if, in some curious sense, she had been expecting this blow. It brings an echo of an earlier tragedy.

SUSAN
A smear? . . . What . . . What kind of smear . . . ? Where are you?

INT. SIDNEY'S APARTMENT – DAY

Steve is on the phone in foreground, the others watching him. In particular, Sally, who stands near Steve, is studying him with obvious sympathy. She looks slowly toward Sidney.

STEVE
(*to the phone*)
We're on our way to the Elysian Room to dicker with Van Cleve – he's fired us already. I'll call you later, dear . . . Bye! . . .

He hangs up quietly, looks at Sidney and walks toward the door.

Come on, Frank.

ANOTHER ANGLE

As the door closes behind Steve, Frank follows, more slowly. As D'Angelo reaches the door, he pauses with his hand on the doorknob and turns back to study Sidney.

SIDNEY

He feels uneasy under D'Angelo's scrutiny. Sally, in background, is also watching Sidney.

SIDNEY
(*to D'Angelo*)
What are you looking at . . .?

103

D'ANGELO

*He does not answer for a moment. The unspoken accusation in his look
is very clear. Then:*

D'ANGELO
(*quietly*)
The ugly world, Sidney . . .
(*a pause*)
If I told Steve what I really think, he'd tear your head off . . .

RESUME SIDNEY

He brazens it out.

SIDNEY
(*sneering*)
Tell him.

RESUME D'ANGELO

D'Angelo shakes his head.

D'ANGELO
No. I'm interested in his future.

D'Angelo goes slowly out.

RESUME SIDNEY

*He hesitates before turning towards Sally (because he realizes that this
exchange with D'Angelo must have confirmed Sally in her
suspicions).*

SALLY

Her face shows that Sidney is right. Sally is deeply hurt, disillusioned.

ANOTHER ANGLE

Sidney turns to her, challenging.

SIDNEY
What's the matter?

SALLY
(*not looking at him*)

Nothing . . .

Resentfully, Sidney moves about the room. Sensing the silent accusation against him, he is aggressive.

SIDNEY

You know, Sally, sometimes I get the impression you think you live in Star-Bright Park. This is life, kid – *get used to it!*

Sidney comes to the phone on her desk. He dials. Then he glances swiftly at Sally and, carrying the phone, walks into the bedroom, dragging the long cord behind him.

SIDNEY
(*calmly, into phone*)

Hello, J. J. . . . I presume you saw the Elwell smear.
(*smiling*)
No, no medals – not yet. Oh, it's worse than that – Aunty Van Cleve is firing them . . . from the horse's mouth . . . They were just here – in a panic . . .

INT. HUNSECKER'S APARTMENT. STUDY – DAY

Hunsecker wears a dressing-gown as he sits at his breakfast table. Behind him are the big glass windows to the terrace overlooking the Manhattan skyline. The papers are at Hunsecker's elbow; his manner is crisp and cold.

HUNSECKER

Who was just there?
(*then*)
You'll be the death of me, Sidalee! Why? Didn't you just tell me that they've already traced this smear to you? All they have to do now is to put two and two together and I'm a chicken in a pot!

RESUME SIDNEY'S APARTMENT

Sidney smiles confidently, answers calmly:

105

SIDNEY

J. J., peace on earth, goodwill to men – it's working out just
the way I planned. Yeah. I guarantee this bomb will pop right
on schedule, but you have to play your part – you be a Saint
and let me be the Devil. But I wanna talk to you first . . .

RESUME HUNSECKER'S APARTMENT

Hunsecker pauses, eyes full of cold voltage.

HUNSECKER

Don't come here, Susie is up and about.
(*listening*)
He called her? You'd better see me at the TV – three
o'clock.

He bangs down the phone, tense but thoughtful in his manner.

INT. CIGAR STAND. LOBBY – DAY

Susan buys paper – dolly with her toward elevator. She gets in.

INT. HUNSECKER'S LIVING ROOM (DEN?)

*J. J. has not moved; he is thoughtful and morose. Nikko, the Japanese
butler, comes in to remove the breakfast table.*

HUNSECKER

The table can wait. No calls. I have to think about my TV
show.

NIKKO

Pleased to do. I will come back later.

HUNSECKER
(*abruptly*)
Did you put the bread out on the terrace for the birds?

NIKKO

Yes, but they don't come no more this time of year.

*Smiling, Nikko leaves. Hunsecker picks up a pencil and makes a note
on a pad, about birds no doubt. Abruptly he looks up, calling:*

HUNSECKER

Susie! Come in a minute, dear . . .

She has been trying to pass unnoticed to her room. She comes forward to him; her manner is serious and wary. His act is one of a tasteful Mammy singer, but he is watchful, too.

Susie, you're very much in my thoughts today.

SUSAN

Why?

HUNSECKER

What a question, dear, with that newspaper in your hand . . .

SUSAN
(pausing)

Did Sidney tell you about it?

HUNSECKER

Yes, he phoned. I don't know this boy too well. Anything in these charges?

She shakes her head.

Not being partial, are you?

                    SUSAN
              (*with quiet certainty*)
No, I'm not. I'm not!

He soothes, smiles, indulgent but watchful:

                  HUNSECKER
Susie, take it easy. I'll trust your judgement – you don't have
to protest with me.

*With a paternal gesture of affection, he hold out his arms, inviting her
into his comforting embrace. Not wanting to, she walks into his open
waiting arms.*

                  HUNSECKER
You know, dear, we're drifting apart, you and I, and I don't
like that.

                    SUSAN
I thought we were talking about Sidney?

                  HUNSECKER
                 (*with rasp*)
Let me finish, dear. You had your say, now let me have
mine . . .

                    SUSAN
                (*interrupting*)
I haven't said anything yet, J. J., but if –

*Susan hesitates. Hunsecker waits for her to continue. But she isn't yet
sure enough of herself or of the point she means to make. She turns
away.*

                  HUNSECKER
                  (*gently*)
I started to say we're drifting apart. A year ago, in your wildest
dreams, would you have walked by that door without taking
up this situation with me? Today I had to call you in!

                    SUSAN
I'm taking up the situation with you now . . .

HUNSECKER
(*interrupting*)

Susie, I want to help you – there's nothing I won't do for you.
You're all I've got in the whole, wide world.

*Hunsecker strides about, elaborately playing on a note of disillusion and
pain.*

It's you who counts, but don't get me wrong – I don't intend
to let you break your neck again!

SUSAN

J. J., you said you want to help me – prove it!

HUNSECKER
(*quietly*)

How?

SUSAN

Get Steve back his job . . . please . . .

HUNSECKER
(*pausing*)

He means that much to you . . .?

SUSAN
(*simply*)

Yes.
(*then*)

With your 'prestige' it only takes a minute – ten cents' worth
of American Tel and Tel.

HUNSECKER

You're picking up my lingo, hon.

SUSAN
(*levelly*)

I read your column every day . . .

*He looks at her with pursed lips and, for a change, some real interest.
Her level, straightforward manner has pinned him down completely; he
shows a slow, charming grin, as he goes for a private phone book.*

HUNSECKER

Susie, I like this new attitude of yours. You're growing up and

I like it! I don't like it when you're limp and dependent, when you're odd and wayward. This gives you a chance for real survival in a very lousy world. Because, don't forget, dear, you won't always have me with you, will you . . .?

SUSAN

No, I won't . . .

He crosses to the white desk phone, delaying dialing for a moment.

HUNSECKER

This Dallas boy must be good for you. Why not bring him around today, before the show? This time I'll clean my glasses for a better look. A man couldn't ask for a squarer shake.

(*into phone*)

Let me have Billy Van Cleve . . .

(*then*)

Don't ever tell anyone, Susie, how I'm tied to your apron strings . . .

(*to phone*)

Billy! J. J.! What's this about that boy? *What* boy? Where are we, lug, in a drawing room comedy? Your brain is warming up, sweetheart – yeah, Dallas! . . .

(*then*)

No, don't explain your point of view, but don't let him go . . .

LAP DISSOLVE TO:

EXT. TV THEATRE – DAY

Camera shoots toward the entrance to the TV theatre. A line of people are queuing for Hunsecker's TV broadcast which is advertised by large posters beside the entrance. A taxi drives up in foreground; Susan Hunsecker gets out.

SIDNEY

Sidney comes up Sixth Avenue towards the theatre. As he reaches the corner of the building, he halts, having seen . . .

SUSAN

*Susan is seen in the act of paying the driver. As the taxi pulls away,
Susan walks camera left.*

TV THEATRE

*Susan pauses, deciding not to enter the theatre; turning she looks about
her and waits on the sidewalk outside.*

SIDNEY

*Sidney decides that this is not the moment to approach Susan. He
glances down the side-street then moves off in that direction.*

SIDE-STREET

*Sidney moves down the side-street toward a stage entrance, through
which are emerging some TV technicians. He slips inside.*

INT. TV STATION – DAY

*Hunsecker is standing at a table, stop-watch in hand, reading aloud
from a script which he is rehearsing and timing. Beside him sits Mary,
busy typing more of the material from Hunsecker's handwritten note.*

*Mary is calm, but he is irritable, trying to concentrate despite the bustle
around him.*

*An old movie star, Mildred Tam, sits waiting in one of the canvas-
backed chairs supplied for the guests on the show.*

SIDNEY

*Shooting toward the auditorium, from Hunsecker's viewpoint. Sidney
mounts the steps onto the stage. Seeing that the columnist is surrounded
but knowing that J. J. wants to talk to him privately, Sidney loiters so
that J. J. can join him as soon as he chooses to. Camera pulls back to
include Hunsecker. Only momentarily distracted by private
considerations connected with Sidney's arrival, Hunsecker returns to the
business of timing the script. He clicks the watch again . . .*

HUNSECKER

'From Washington through to Jefferson, from Lincoln and
F.D.R. right up to today – the Democratic Way of Life!
That's what the man said! Nowadays it doesn't export too
well . . .
                    (*then, concluding*)
But you know . . . and I know . . . that our best secret
weapon is D-E-M-O-C-R-A-C-Y.
                    (*dropping to a modest tone*)
Let's never forget it, ladies and gentlemen.'

ANOTHER ANGLE

*Sidney lingers beside the old movie star who is listening, rapt, to
Hunsecker's words. Sidney is less impressed with J. J.'s eloquence. At
the conclusion, Mildred applauds lightly. She stands up and moves
towards Hunsecker. Hunsecker wants to talk to Sidney but is frustrated
by the old movie star.*

MILDRED TAM

That's grand, just grand, J. J.!
                    (*then, anxiously*)
Is my make-up all right? You know, despite the scads of
movies I've made, I've never appeared on TV yet . . .

HUNSECKER
                    (*cutting her short*)
Of course, Mildred. Of course. You look fine.
                    (*swiftly summoning Mary*)
Mary, help Miss Tam – anything she wants; she's our star
today.

*Under the pretense of studying the typed script, J. J. walks away across
the stage. Sidney strolls after him.*

ANOTHER ANGLE

*A tracking shot. Sidney comes up beside Hunsecker, falls into step beside
him. As they cross toward a water cooler at the back of the stage, they
talk in rapid undertone.*

HUNSECKER

I got that boy coming over here. If I can trust my eyes, and I
think I can, Susie knows all about your dirty work.

SIDNEY
(*shrugging*)

Can't hurt . . .

HUNSECKER
(*incredulously*)

Can't hurt? I had to get him back his job.

SIDNEY
(*closer, faster*)

Look, J. J., we can wrap this up in one neat bundle, addressed
to the dumps – to *oblivion*. We're going great, but please play
it my way. I cased this kid. Know his ins and outs . . . He's
fulla juice and vinegar, just begging for some big shot like you
to give him a squeeze. Do little Sidney a favor: squeeze! You
know, J. J. – the porcupine bit – *needles*.

HUNSECKER

But it's too late. I got him back the job . . .

SIDNEY
(*impatiently*)

No, that's the point – he won't accept your favor! The
manager yes, but not the *boy*.

A pause. Hunsecker renumerates.

HUNSECKER

What's this boy got that Susie likes?

SIDNEY

Integrity – acute, like indigestion.

HUNSECKER

What does that mean – integrity?

SIDNEY
(*repeating as before*)

A pocket fulla firecrackers – looking for a match!

(*grinning*)
It's a new wrinkle to tell the truth . . . I never thought I'd
make a killing on some guy's 'integrity'.

Hunsecker gives him certain slow begrudging admiration.

HUNSECKER
I'd hate to take a bite of you; you're a cookie full of arsenic.

*Sidney smirks. He turns away and goes off toward the auditorium in
the background.*

EXT. TV STATION – DAY

*Frank D'Angelo pays a taxi out of which he and Steve have just
emerged. Frank turns toward the boy, resuming a conversation as they
stroll across the sidewalk toward the entrance of the theatre.*

STEVE
(*depressed*)
I still think he's responsible for the smear.

D'ANGELO
Not that I'm convinced, but you'll never prove it in a million
years.
(*gently*)
Steve, you'll do what you want, but it can't hurt; he offers you
an olive branch – so today *like olives!*

D'Angelo stops, halted by an expression which he sees in Steve's face.

STEVE

*He is looking through the glass doors of the TV theatre, no longer
listening to D'Angelo's words; his face has hardened in anger.*

INT. TV THEATRE FOYER – DAY

*From Steve's viewpoint. Sidney has come out of the curtained entrance
to the auditorium. Camera pulls back to include Steve in foreground.
With a movement that suggests his annoyance at discovering Sidney
present, Steve jerks open the glass door and moves in.*

ANOTHER ANGLE

Susan is waiting in the foyer. She is standing in a position where she has not been able to see Steve until he enters; now she moves forward to greet him. As soon as she is near him, she speaks in a quiet, urgent manner.

> SUSAN
> *(in an undertone)*
> Steve, before we go in – I'd like to . . .

But she, too, is halted as Steve lays a hand on her arm. Seeing his look over her shoulder, she turns . . .

SIDNEY

He is already strolling forward to join them. Camera pans with him to include Susie, Steve and D'Angelo.

> SIDNEY
> Hey, Susie – This is a real surprise – not one but three. J. J.'s just finishing up his rehearsal.

STAGE

Hunsecker comes forward to the front of the stage looking toward . . .

STEVE, SUSAN, D'ANGELO AND SIDNEY

The group comes down the aisle of the empty theatre.

RESUME HUNSECKER

He studies them, then calls out:

> HUNSECKER
> Looks like a wedding.

REVERSE ANGLE

Hunsecker – back to camera in foreground. He begins to whistle 'The Wedding March' to the rhythm of Steve's and Susan's walk.

STEVE

He breaks the rhythm of his stride, his face rigid.

RESUME HUNSECKER

He descends to meet them; his manner is full of welcome.

REVERSE ANGLE

Susan nervously makes the introduction – Steve is nervous; D'Angelo hangs behind warily; Sidney is in background.

SUSAN
Steve, you remember my brother . . .

STEVE AND HUNSECKER
(*together*)
Of course.

Steve shakes the hand that the smiling Hunsecker gives.

HUNSECKER
Well, son, looks like you went out and bought yourself a packet of trouble . . .

STEVE
You've been very kind about it, Mr Hunsecker.

HUNSECKER
Give Susie credit for that. I took her word that there was nothing to the smear. Matter of fact, I'll have my say about smears on the show today. That's why I'd like *your* personal assurance, too.

STEVE
(*quietly*)
Mr Hunsecker, there's nothing to that smear. You have my
· sincere word . . .

HUNSECKER
(*nodding judicially*)
I'll buy that, son. Now, you owe *me* a favor.

> (*pausing; to Susan*)
Be good to my kid sister . . .

SIDNEY
(*solemnly*)
Yeah, she's had a peck of trouble for a kid . . .

Hunsecker flicks a look at Sidney. The others, warier by the minute, remain silent. Hunsecker purrs onward.

HUNSECKER
Susie likes to keep her girlish secrets. But in her heart of hearts I imagine, Dallas, that she fancies you in an uncommon way. Now, what about *you*, son? Not just tomcatting around . . . I hope?

SUSAN
(*quickly*)
J. J., Steve isn't . . .

Hunsecker cuts her off with lazy good nature.

HUNSECKER
Take it easy, Susie. He wouldn't be much of man if he didn't understand my concern. Would you, son?

STEVE
(*pausing, quietly*)
No, I wouldn't . . .

HUNSECKER
(*nodding*)
Serious as a deacon . . . I like it. I like your style, son! In a world of old rags and bones, I like it! For instance, take Sidney.

Hunsecker crosses toward Sidney.

If Sidney got anywhere near Susie I'd break a bat over Sidney's head!
> (*smiling faintly*)
Sidney lives so much in a moral twilight that, when I said you were coming here, he predicted disaster. You wouldn't take

my favor – you'd chew up the job, he said, and spit it right
back in my face!
> (*sniffing*)

Any truth in that . . .?

D'ANGELO, STEVE AND SUSAN

Steve is thrown momentarily; Frank steps in.

> ### D'ANGELO
No, Mr Hunsecker, and if I can amplify –

> ### HUNSECKER
> (*motionless*)

Don't amplify.

RESUME D'ANGELO, STEVE AND SUSAN

> ### D'ANGELO
Steve wantsa thank you for this favor. He –

GROUP SHOT

> ### SIDNEY
> (*provocatively*)

Frank, you don't listen! J. J. just told you to shut your mouth!

> ### STEVE
> (*hotly*)

Don't you think it's about time you shut yours? Who are you
to tell a man like Frank D'Angelo to shut up?!

> ### FRANK
> (*warningly*)

Steve, that isn't important –

But Steve, on a heated rip, has turned to Hunsecker.

> ### STEVE
Does he have to be here in our hair?

HUNSECKER

HUNSECKER
Why, has he bothered you before?

STEVE, D'ANGELO AND SUSAN

STEVE
Is it news to you?

HUNSECKER

HUNSECKER
Son, lots of people tell me I'm a gifted man, but I still can't see around corners.

GROUP SHOT

HUNSECKER
(*tolerantly*)
Just exactly what are you so hot about?
(*waiting*)
I mean, I know it's a difficult thing to be an artist in this crudest of possible worlds, but –

STEVE
(*impatiently*)
Nuts! I'm not here as an artist! I'm here as an average Joe, who happens to love your sister Susie!

HUNSECKER
(*with ironic smirk*)
Well, just be careful you don't knock her down, huh?

Steve stops dead. Then, strangely and dangerously, he picks up Hunsecker's smile. On each man's face the smile broadens and grows up into a chuckle from each; but the meanness still flickers around Hunsecker's mouth. Steve is out of the net!

(*affably*)
Frankly, son, you lost me on that last hill. Just give us the punch line . . .

STEVE
(*agreeably*)
No punch line. Maybe I was just admiring your know-how –
yours and Falco's.

HUNSECKER AND SIDNEY

HUNSECKER
Why do you keep coupling me with Falco?

STEVE, D'ANGELO AND SUSAN

STEVE
(*innocently*)
He's here, isn't he? Do you think, sir, when he dies he'll go to
the dog and cat heaven?

HUNSECKER AND SIDNEY

*Even Hunsecker smiles. Sidney likes neither the ridicule nor the turn of
events. He moves quickly past camera.*

SIDNEY, STEVE, D'ANGELO AND SUSAN

Sidney comes round the row of theater seats to attack Steve.

SIDNEY
Let's forget cats and dogs and other pseudo-literary remarks –
I'll just lay it on the line! What about that big rumpus in my
office today? You were there, Frank! Where, according to St
Dallas, J. J. was responsible for the Elwell smear!

HUNSECKER

HUNSECKER
Don't go wild, Sidney.

GROUP SHOT

SIDNEY
Wild? Take a look at them and see who's wild . . .

121

Playing along nicely, Hunsecker looks at Steve and Frank and slowly removes his arm from Susan; he pauses before asking Dallas:

> HUNSECKER
>
> What about that . . .?

> D'ANGELO
> (*uneasily*)
>
> Steve was excited . . . he didn't mean it exactly the way it's stated here . . .

> HUNSECKER
> (*to Steve*)
>
> How did you mean it . . .?
> (*simultaneously*)

SIDNEY	SUSAN
What he likes to –	J. J., I don't want to say –

With a roar Hunsecker takes them both out of play; he stands up.

SIDNEY, STEVE, D'ANGELO

Hunsecker enters from behind camera.

> HUNSECKER
>
> Both of you keep quiet! If your're tired, Susie, sit down – This needs investigation!
> (*to Steve, quieter*)
> How did you mean it . . .?
> (*waiting*)
> Come on, let's go! Let's go! . . .

Steve is cornered, the other completely out of play. He pauses.

> STEVE
>
> I don't take kindly to you and Falco selling me ethics. Who's the injured party here, you?

> HUNSECKER
> (*with contempt*)
>
> Right now you're in no position to ask questions! And your snide remarks –

STEVE
(*stronger*)

Wait a minute, I haven't handed over punishing privileges to you *yet*! Put the whip down and I might respect what you're saying . . .

Switching his leonine tail, Hunsecker looks broodingly at Susan. Frank says one beseeching word, 'Steve . . . ', but no one hears him.

HUNSECKER

Susie, did you know about this accusation . -. .?

SUSAN

SUSAN
(*mutely*)

No . . .

HUNSECKER

HUNSECKER
(*abruptly*)
Before you leave, son, I'll answer your question – Susan
Hunsecker is the injured party here!
(*balefully*)
Or will I be hearing next that I don't even have my sister's
welfare at heart . . .

STEVE AND SUSAN

*Steve hesitates defensively but can't resist a small smile; he moves nearer
to Susan.*

STEVE
Mr Hunsecker, you've got more twists than a barrel of
pretzels.

HUNSECKER
(*unturning*)
You hear that, Susie . . .
(*to Steve*)
Continue please . . .

STEVE
(*shaking his head*)
I'm afraid I can't cope with them.

REVERSE ANGLE

Susan in foreground, Steve, Hunsecker and Sidney beyond.

STEVE
(*simply*)
You're too shrewd for me so I'll just be honest. Susie and I
love each other, if I'm not mistaken, and we want to get
married.

Hunsecker pauses; Sidney throws in a stage whisper:

SIDNEY
Give him credit – the boy's gall is gorgeous!

STEVE

Why don't we hear what Susie has to say?

HUNSECKER
(*sardonically*)

That's stout of you, Dallas, but Susie may not care to air her
dismal views in public . . .

*Steve walks to Susie, trying to lift her with his hopes and air of gentle
urging and support.*

STEVE

Susie . . .?

SUSAN

She stares at the floor.

RESUME REVERSE ANGLE

*Hunsecker doesn't like the drift of things; his mouth tightens and he
speaks to Susan with veiled warning:*

HUNSECKER

Susie, as always, is free to say anything she thinks. Go on,
dear, say exactly what's on your mind, dear.

STEVE

Those 'dears' sound like daggers. May I suggest that you stop
daring her to speak?

HUNSECKER

May I lift my eyebrows? What is this? What are you trying to
do?

STEVE
(*strongly*)

I'm trying to get Susie to stand up to you. But your manner is
so threatening that she's afraid to speak!

HUNSECKER

Son, you raise your voice again and – !

SUSAN

Suddenly Susan lets loose.

                              SUSAN

Please! Please! Stop! . . . J. J.? –

HUNSECKER

He interjects.

                           HUNSECKER
                             (*contritely*)

Susie, I'm sorry if –

RESUME SUSAN

Restraining tears, she runs up the steps to the stage.

STEVE, HUNSECKER AND SIDNEY

Steve looks after her. Sidney watches intently. Hunsecker's smile is frostily taunting.

                           HUNSECKER

We may have to call this game on account of darkness . . .

Steve turns a blank-eyed stare at him. Tension gone, a slow mumbling fatigue has set in. Hunsecker plays it light.

If looks could kill, I'm dead . . .

                              STEVE
                             (*slowly*)

No, I don't care about you – you're fantastic. My whole interest, if it's not too late, is in Susie . . . and how to undo what you've done to her . . .

                           HUNSECKER
                            (*smiling*)

And what have I done to her, besides not buying her a new fur coat lately? Sidney, you were right – the boy's a dilly.

STEVE
(*stung*)

Why? Because I don't like the way you *toy* with human lives?
– Your contempt and malice? Because I won't be the
accomplice of your sick ego – and the way it's crippled
Susie . . .? You think of yourself – you and your column –
you see yourself as a national glory . . . but to me, and
thousands of others like me, you and your slimy scandal, your
phony patriotics – to me, Mr Hunsecker you *are a national
disgrace*!

HUNSECKER
(*blandly*)

Son, I don't fancy shooting mosquitoes with elephant guns.
So suppose you just shuffle along and call it a day . . .

He turns and starts away, but Steve stops him with –

STEVE

But my day with Susie isn't over yet and –

HUNSECKER
(*cold*)

Here's your head. What's your hurry?

STAGE

*Hunsecker comes up the steps from the auditorium, Sidney following
closely behind. In background, beyond, Steve and D'Angelo are
walking up the aisle to the exit. Camera tracks close on Sidney and
Hunsecker. Hunsecker's face is rigid. Sidney, close at his elbow,
whispers:*

SIDNEY
(*softly*)

You did it, J. J., you did it good . .

*Sidney is full of confidence. But Hunsecker barely hears him. Hunsecker
has been hurt very deeply by the boy's attack; in particular, by the
appalling fear that what Steve has said is the kind of thing which
Susan may also secretly believe.*

ANOTHER ANGLE

Susan is still standing in the wings. Mary is with her, obviously sympathetic.

HUNSECKER

Again we see some emotion in his face as he studies the girl. His eyes flick toward the stage behind him where Sidney stands watching. He moves gently forward and then speaks in a quiet voice which reveals how desperately he needs her reassurance.

HUNSECKER

Susie . . . I . . . I'd have to take it very much amiss if you ever saw that boy again.

SUSAN

After a pause, she turns toward him; she looks him straight in the face.

SUSAN
(*levelly*)

I'll never see him again.

RESUME HUNSECKER

He seems to take this as a gesture of forgiveness from her. Now he touches her. His need for her is apparent; he tries to reach her, tries to find an excuse to embrace her. She submits to this very passively.

SUSAN

A very close shot. We see the effort with which she is controlling herself.

RESUME TWO SHOT

Satisfied with this crumb of affection from his sister, Hunsecker lets her go. Susan moves away, still avoiding his eyes. Then she goes off toward the steps down into the auditorium. Sidney looks at Hunsecker, then after Susan and follows her.

RESUME HUNSECKER

He goes back to Mary and the script. He instructs her:

128

HUNSECKER

Call Van Cleve. Tell him he was right. Tell him I said the Dallas boys are not worthy of his club.

Mary says nothing.

Hunsecker gathers his papers and with a visible effort to resume his public personality turns toward the machinery of the television broadcast in background.

EXT. TV THEATRE – DAY

Susan comes running out calling:

SUSAN

Taxi!

SIDNEY

He comes out after her.

SIDNEY

Susie!

SUSAN

She has already opened the door of a taxi at the curb. She turns, sees Sidney coming up behind her, quickly enters the cab.

ANOTHER ANGLE

As Sidney steps up, he grasps at the door of the taxi, trying to hold it open, but Susan pulls it shut, catching his fingers in the door. Sidney steps back in pain.

TAXI

It drives off down Sixth Avenue.

SIDNEY

Nursing the injury to his hand, he looks after the disappearing taxi.

DISSOLVE TO:

INT. DINING ROOM. TWENTY-ONE CLUB

Two waiters are fussing over Hunsecker's table at which places are already set for Sidney and Hunsecker. Maître d' hands him an envelope as he passes.

MAÎTRE D'

Mr Hunsecker, this was to be delivered to you personally –

When the columnist comes up to the table, the waiters quickly pull out the table for him. Sidney comes to join him; Sidney gets some attention, but considerably less. Camera moves closer.

HUNSECKER

These drinks are warm.

WAITER

You said you like to have them on your table.

HUNSECKER

What are you, a critic?

WAITER

I'll change –

HUNSECKER

Forget it.

SIDNEY

We're on the verge of a farce, a real farce. As I see it, if Susie had stood behind him today he might have proved a threat. But since primarily he's wedded to his work, he's not going to be able to take it.

A Waiter shifts the position of the salad dish at Hunsecker's elbow.

HUNSECKER
(*to Waiter*)

Stop tinkering, pal – that horseradish won't jump a fence!

The Waiter retreats rapidly.

SIDNEY

In brief, J. J., it's all over because any hour now the boy will give *her* up. Is it a farce or not?

Delicately salting his oysters, Hunsecker looks obliquely at Sidney.

> **HUNSECKER**
> This syrup you're giving out, Sidney, you pour over waffles, not J. J. Hunsecker! What do you mean that lousy kid will give up my sister?

Hunsecker with a casual gesture, tugs lightly at the end of Sidney's tie. Hunsecker's gesture is playful, but it inflicts great injury to Sidney's dignity; Sidney cannot bear to be touched; he finds this liberty on J. J.'s part as intolerable as anything he has experienced and only with great difficulty controls himself. The shot favors Sidney.

SIDNEY AND HUNSECKER

Hunsecker continues.

> **HUNSECKER**
> Are you listening?

SIDNEY
(*warily*)
How does it matter who's sister? The main thing, they're
through and –

HUNSECKER

From Sidney's viewpoint. Without turning, Hunsecker interrupts.

HUNSECKER
Am I supposed to forget how that boy talked to me today?

RESUME SIDNEY AND HUNSECKER

Sidney senses a warning in Hunsecker's manner. He protests.

SIDNEY
J. J., is he worthy of a second glance from a man like you? Is
he, I mean? . . .

HUNSECKER

*From Sidney's viewpoint. Pausing during the process of eating,
Hunsecker reaches into an inside pocket.*

HUNSECKER
Bite on this.

*Camera pulls back to include Sidney as Hunsecker tosses in front of him
an envelope. Sidney opens it, extracts two steamship tickets.*

SIDNEY
Steamship tickets?

HUNSECKER
(*as he eats*)
For the next sailing of the *Mary*. Susan's run down.

*Sidney slowly pushes the envelope back to Hunsecker, who leaves it
lying on the table before him.*

SIDNEY
That's good. Now that louse is outa Susie's hair for good.

133

SIDNEY

He has an instinct to laugh; but something tells him not to.

HUNSECKER

As Sidney makes no response, Hunsecker slowly, carefully continues in a voice which is dangerously soft.

                    HUNSECKER
        I want that boy taken apart.

SIDNEY AND HUNSECKER

Shooting across Hunsecker onto Sidney. Sidney puts down his fork. He sees now that the issue is serious and must be faced.

                    SIDNEY
                    (*seriously*)
        Why do something that would drive them right back into each
        other's arms?

HUNSECKER

He wants no advice from Sidney. He interrupts with quiet savagery.

                    HUNSECKER
        I know how to handle Susie. You just handle the boy,
        Sidney . . .
                    (*scribbles on scratch pad*)
        . . . preferably tonight.
                    (*pushes pad across to Sidney*)

SIDNEY AND HUNSECKER

Shooting across Hunsecker onto Sidney. Sidney feels sick.

                    SIDNEY
        Why, what's tomorrow – a holiday?

Camera moves closer as Sidney picks up scratch pad. We can read two words: 'Get Kello'.

        I think I'll go home – maybe I left my sense of humor in
        another suit.

134

HUNSECKER

Hunsecker finishes eating. During the ensuing speech, which he begins quietly and sensibly, Hunsecker's venomous feelings are unexpectedly betrayed.

HUNSECKER

You've got that God-given brain – learn to use it! Do you think it's a personal matter with me, this boy? Are you telling me I see things in terms of personal pique? Don't you see that today that boy wiped his feet on the choice, on the predilections of sixty million men and women of the greatest country in the world! If you had any morals yourself, you would understand the immorality of that boy's stand today! It was not me he criticized – it was my readers! . . .

Camera pulls back to include Sidney. Hunsecker manages to control himself; he reaches with nervous fingers toward his scribbling pad.

HUNSECKER AND SIDNEY

Shooting across Sidney onto Hunsecker.

HUNSECKER
(*a quiet warning*)

Don't remove the gangplank, Sidney; you may wanna get back on board.

Shooting across Hunsecker onto Sidney. A waiter has come to serve the next course. Hunsecker appears relaxed, but Sidney is sightlessly staring at the piece of paper in his hand. He speaks with a quaver in his voice, for he has worked hard to make a life which he is now ready to relinquish.

SIDNEY

J. J., it's one thing to wear your dog collar . . . but when it gets to be a noose . . . I'd rather have my freedom.

HUNSECKER

The man in jail is always for freedom.

Sidney begins to get up from the table.

SIDNEY
(*as he rises*)
Except, if you'll excuse me, I'm not in jail.

Hunsecker looks up at Sidney.

HUNSECKER

From Sidney's viewpoint.

HUNSECKER
(*easily*)
Sure you're in jail, Sidney. You're a prisoner of your own
fears, of your own greed and ambition; you're in jail.

SIDNEY

He looks down on Hunsecker, leans over the table.

SIDNEY
You're blind, Mr Magoo. This is a crossroads for me. I won't
get Kello. Not for a lifetime pass to the Polo Grounds. Not if
you serve me Cleopatra on a plate.

*Camera has pulled back to include Hunsecker, whose attention has
returned to his food.*

HUNSECKER
(*over-patient*)
Sidney, I told you –

SIDNEY
(*continuing*)
J. J., I swear to you on my mother's life, I won't do it.
(*he leans even closer*)
If you gave me your column I wouldn't do a thing like
that . . .

*But as he speaks the last words, Sidney's voice falters because he has
glanced down at the table . . .*

SIDNEY

We see that an idea has entered his head – an idea that takes the wind out of his indignation. His eyes lift rapidly to Hunsecker's face.

> HUNSECKER
> (*delicately touching the envelope*)
> And who do you think writes the column while Susie and I
> are away for three months? . . .

RESUME SIDNEY

He is quite speechless. Over scene Hunsecker's voice:

> HUNSECKER
> (*off-screen*)
> . . . The man in the moon?

HUNSECKER AND SIDNEY

*Camera shoots across Sidney again onto Hunsecker. Hunsecker leans
back, looks at Sidney. Seeing that Sidney has accepted the proposition,
he smiles.*

> HUNSECKER
> (*softly*)
> Thank you, Sidney.

*In a pleasantly affable way, he leans across the table to tap the hand
with which Sidney is leaning on the table.*

> And, Sidney, I'll have that piece of paper back . . .

*Helplessly, Sidney unclenches a fist and reveals the slip of paper which
he had meant to keep. Hunsecker takes it. With his eyes on Sidney, he
slowly tears it up . . .*

LAP DISSOLVE TO:

INT. CAFÉ OFF LOBBY OF (HUNSECKER'S) BRILL BUILDING –
NIGHT

*The dining counter is deserted, except for the counterman, who appears
to be getting ready to close. Steve and Susan enter from the corridor. She
is wearing her fur coat about her shoulders like a cloak. They are both
in a deeply serious mood as they seat themselves at the counter.*

STEVE
(*to counterman*)
Two coffees . . .

SUSAN AND STEVE

*A closer angle. They will talk in quiet undertones, their voices heavy
with sadness. Susan is close to hopelessness and despair. Steve is
sympathetic, but not without determination. They barely touch the coffee
mugs placed before them.*

SUSAN
(*haltingly*)
Steve . . . I love the way you stood up to my brother . . . but
it frightened me . . .

STEVE
Is that why you walked out?

SUSAN
(*pathetically*)
Yes . . . What you say to me . . . it's true. I'm weak. I can't
change.

STEVE
(*softly*)
I gather . . . you're trying to say goodbye.

SUSAN
(*wrenches it out*)
Yes . . .

STEVE
I came here with half an idea of saying goodbye, but I guess
I'll hang around . . . to *plead* . . .
(*he looks at her for a long time*)
Susie . . . is this really what you want?

SUSAN
Yes. My brother is capable of doing very great harm and I
can't let that happen. We can't –

STEVE
(*interrupting*)

I won't give you up . . .

SUSAN

– We can't see each other again . . .

STEVE
(*flaring*)

That's fish four days old! Susie, I won't buy it! Right out of
that mouth I love like a ventriloquist's dummy your *brother* is
saying goodbye!

SUSAN
(*holding her head in her hands*)

No, Steve. Please don't. Please don't. At least this way I'll
know that you'll be somewhere in the world alive, happy,
working . . .

STEVE
(*unyielding*)
I won't give you up.

SUSAN
(*quietly, but with finality*)
You've got to go.

She gets up from the counter, goes toward the door, with Steve following. Her fur coat starts to slip off. Steve puts it back on her.

STEVE
This coat is your brother. I've always hated this coat.

Susan moves toward the exit into the hallway. Steve follows.

HALLWAY

Frank D'Angelo is waiting for them. Silently they come up to join him, depressed. Susan looks at D'Angelo a little pathetically.

SUSAN
Goodbye, Mr D'Angelo. Take care of Steve.

D'Angelo nods, tips his hat and walks a little way down the corridor, leaving them alone again.

SUSAN AND STEVE

She looks at him, trying to smile, trying to make a joke.

SUSAN
Say something funny . . . Mr Hasenpfeffer.

Steve steps to her quickly, kisses her. Then he turns and swiftly walks off down the corridor without a backward glance. He goes past D'Angelo, who walks quietly after him toward the exit in background.

SUSAN

She remains just in the attitude in which Steve left her.

EXT. BRILL BUILDING – NIGHT

Steve comes out of the door, pauses without looking back. D'Angelo comes up behind him.

140

STEVE
                (*after a moment*)
    Look back, Frank. See if she's still standing there.

D'Angelo looks discreetly over his shoulder.

    SUSAN

From D'Angelo's point of view. She is still standing where Steve left her.

    RESUME STEVE AND D'ANGELO

                    D'ANGELO
    She's still standing there.

Steve, still without looking back, walks away.

    LAP DISSOLVE TO:

EXT. JOE ROBARD'S CLUB – NIGHT

A long shot of the club exterior, framing the outline of the bridge against the night sky in background. From inside comes the sound of music – the quintet. A black car comes swiftly under the bridge, turns into the little square opposite the club, braking sharply.

    CLOSER ANGLE

As the car comes to a stop, camera shoots across the hood onto the windshield where we see the insignia: police. The occupants of the car are not visible.

INT. ROBARD'S CLUB – NIGHT

Sidney, standing inside the entrance without overcoat, sees the police car, turns and moves with tense expression through the club past the Steve Dallas Quintet on the stand, toward the bar.

    AT THE BAR

Sidney arrives, orders a Coke. Near him, Joe Robard stands talking to some patrons. Frank D'Angelo is seen approaching from the interior of

the club. Behind him, Dallas and his men can be seen playing.
D'Angelo comes up to Robard, interrupts him.

> D'ANGELO
> Excuse me, Joe, Steve don't feel too good –

> ROBARD
> (*interjecting*)
> I'm sorry to hear it . . .

REVERSE ANGLE

Camera shoots past D'Angelo and Robard in foreground, toward
Sidney who overhears.

> D'ANGELO
> – So, if you don't mind, he'll leave after this set.

In background, Sidney sets down his drink, reacting to this information.
Robard clamps D'Angelo on the shoulder with warm reassurance.

> ROBARD
> I like that boy, Frank. Anything he wants to do is okay with
> me.

> D'ANGELO
> Thanks.

SIDNEY

Thinking rapidly, Sidney leaves the bar, moves unobtrusively but
purposefully towards the coat-rack near the entrance, where Steve
Dallas' easily recognizable black-and-white checked raglan overcoat
can be seen hanging. Sidney takes his own coat and, as he thrusts his
arm into the sleeve, he contrives neatly to slip some unseen object into the
pocket of Steve's overcoat – camera noting this action in a brief, inserted
close shot. From off-screen, a voice suddenly addresses Sidney.

> D'ANGELO'S VOICE
> Hey! . . .

Close-up of Sidney. As he turns in swift apprehension, we see the
moment of panic in his face.

142

REVERSE ANGLE

Camera shoots past Sidney in foreground toward D'Angelo, who advances on Sidney. D'Angelo's manner is unfriendly, and for an instant we feel, like Sidney, that D'Angelo may have seen Sidney tampering with Steve's coat. But then we are reassured as D'Angelo, deliberately using Sidney's surname, says:

> D'ANGELO
> (*continuing*)
> . . . Mr Falco . . . I hate to give you this satisfaction – they broke it off tonight for good.

REVERSE ANGLE

Shooting across D'Angelo onto Sidney, who now relaxes, his fears ungrounded.

> Tell that to Hunsecker – tell him we agree – he's a big man – *he wins all the marbles!*

SIDNEY

As D'Angelo moves away again Sidney looks after him. Once more his face goes tense.

ANOTHER ANGLE

Camera moves with Sidney as he walks toward the doorway. There he hesitates again; he looks back into the club.

DALLAS

From Sidney's viewpoint. A long shot of Steve on the bandstand. Camera pans deliberately towards the coat-rack in foreground. A group of newly arrived musicians walk into the shot, setting down their instrument cases and starting to hang up their coats. (Clearly, Sidney could not now return to the coat-rack – even if he decided that he did want to undo his handiwork.)

RESUME SIDNEY

Camera, shooting out across the square, frames Sidney in foreground.

Facing the inevitable, Sidney turns away, walks across the sidewalk. On the other side of the square the headlamps of the car blink twice. Sidney walks toward it.

EXT. POLICE CAR – NIGHT

A big man gets out of the seat next to the driver. As he comes round the hood of the car, the headlamps of a passing truck illuminate him, identifying Harry Kello. Camera pans as he walks to meet Sidney.

CLOSER ANGLE

Kello pauses as Sidney comes up to him, asks affably:

> KELLO
> What's all the rush? You said three o'clock.

> SIDNEY
> *(glancing back toward club)*
> He's leaving early. After this 'set'. He'll be out in a couple of minutes . . .

> KELLO
> *(heavily humorous)*
> It's nice, Sidney, that you give me this tip . . .

> SIDNEY
> *(interjecting)*
> He's got them on him.

> KELLO
> *(solemnly nodding his approval)*
> . . . And he's got them on him. I appreciate a thing like that – I appreciate where you are looking out for the virtue of the city.

Sidney, annoyed at this sarcasm, moves past Kello, not deigning to respond. As he goes by, Kello grasps him forcibly by the arm.

> KELLO
> What's your hurry, Snooks?

Camera has panned to shoot toward the car out of which emerges a second detective.

SIDNEY
(*revolted*)
Take your hands off, Kello . . .

Kello, holding Sidney, turns toward the second detective in background.

KELLO
Murph, how do you like this face? Why, I'll be darned – it's
melting! Something got you scared, Sidney . . .? Listen,
rectify me a certain thing. Wasn't you kidding, Snooks, when
you told J. J. I was fat . . .?

*Sidney jerks his arm away, rapidly retreats a few yards, a safe distance
from Kello. Camera pans with him to the bottom of the steps.*

SIDNEY
Sleep in peace, Kello – you're skinny – but J. J. says you
sweat!

ANOTHER ANGLE

*Sidney in foreground, Kello and Murph beyond. Kello laughs; but
obviously he would like to be nearer to Sidney. Perhaps to detain
Sidney, Kello drawls:*

KELLO
Is that a fact? He's a dilly, ain't he?

KELLO

He moves forward a little.

KELLO
(*softly now*)
I get the peculiar impression, Snooks, that you don't like me.
Could I be wrong?

SIDNEY
(*as he goes*)
You could be *right*, you fat slob!

145

ANOTHER ANGLE

From halfway up the stairs. Sidney comes up the steps two at a time. Kello and Murph are seen beyond.

KELLO
(*with a guffaw*)
Come back here, Sidney . . . I wanna chastise you! . . .

FROM THE BRIDGE

Sidney reaches the top. He comes along the pedestrian walk up to camera, slowing down he turns across the rail and looks down toward the square. Camera moves to take in the scene in wide angle: Sidney in foreground, the police car and detectives below, the entrance to Robard's across the square. Sidney waits. In the distance we can hear the music of Dallas' last number coming to an end.

INT. ROBARD'S CLUB

The last bars of the number. Enthusiastic applause.

Steve responds to the applause, nicely but a little wearily. He gets down from the stand, starts through the club carrying his guitar.

BRIEF SHOT – THE BANDSTAND

Chico Hamilton and the boys start another number.

EXT. ROBARD'S – NIGHT

Steve emerges from the club wearing his checked overcoat and carrying his guitarcase.

FROM THE BRIDGE

Camera pans from the small figure of Steve to include Sidney big in foreground. Below him Kello and Murph turn toward the club.

KELLO

Closer angle downward from Sidney's viewpoint. Kello turns deliberately to look at the bridge above.

146

RESUME BRIDGE

Sidney sees Kello's look; he nods deliberately. Below him we see Kello and Murph move swiftly to get into the car. Sidney, as if shrinking from a sight which he doesn't wish to witness, draws back from the balustrade. He turns and begins to walk toward camera.

POLICE CAR

A low angle shooting upwards at the car, the stairs to the bridge in background. As the doors of the car slam, it starts to move forward and, abruptly, its headlamps are switched on, glaring into the lens.

EXT. ROBARD'S – NIGHT

Steve, concerned only with his melancholy thoughts, walks down the sidewalk under the bridge. The car headlamps illuminate him in their glare as they move across him. Steve, without undue interest, glances back but continues on his way.

Camera shoots eastward toward the silhouette of the bridge. The police car turns as it comes out of the square under the bridge toward camera. It moves slowly; again its headlamps flare into the lens. Camera pulling back includes Steve in foreground. Behind him the police car slows down at the curb; it barely stops as Kello slips out of the off-side door; then the car moves forward along the curb leaving him behind Steve. As the car goes out of picture past camera, Kello strolls across the sidewalk, following Steve. Steve, looking past camera, notices . . .

REVERSE ANGLE

Camera shoots toward Second Avenue. The police car slows down again at the curb and Murph gets out of it, turning to face Steve.

RESUME STEVE

Steve, seeing the man ahead of him, notes something slightly menacing in his manner and slows down in his walk. Then, instinctively, he realizes that there is a second man behind him, turns to look at Kello. Kello approaches.

KELLO

Hey, fella! . . .

Camera moves closer and closer on Steve. In his face we see a growing sense of something wrong . . .

INT. ROBARD'S CLUB

JUMP CUT. *Loud noise, Chico Hamilton on the drums . . .*

DISSOLVE TO:

INT. BAR OF TOOTS SHOR'S RESTAURANT – LATER

Sidney is at the bar, surrounded by drinkers. Their voices, and his, suggest high spirits, celebration. A Captain is approaching.

DRINKER

I propose a toast! Whaddaya say, huh?

SIDNEY
(*to bartender*)

Three scotches, one vodka and orange juice, and give him an old-fashioned . . .

CAPTAIN
(*taps Sidney*)

Sidney . . . Sidney, there's a phone call for you.

SIDNEY
(*turns to him*)

Lou, I told you, I'm not taking any calls. I don't care who calls, no calls . . .

The Captain goes off.

DRINKER

I still wanna make a toast!

SIDNEY
(*getting a drink from the bartender*)

I'm buying the booze, so I'm making the toast . . .
(*turns, raises his glass*)

Here's to the thing we always dream about. It makes you cool in the summertime, it keeps you hot in the wintertime, it gets you good cooking . . .

Herbie Temple is approaching the bar.

DRINKER

Hey, how ya been?

TEMPLE

Sidney!

SIDNEY

Hello, Charlie . . . How are ya?

TEMPLE

I'm Herbie Temple, remember? The funniest man in town . . .

The Captain is coming back to Sidney.

SIDNEY

Gentlemen, I'm toasting my favorite new perfume . . . Success!

CAPTAIN

She said it was important. The operator at Twenty-One took the message.

SIDNEY

Lou, I'm not taking any messages unless it's J. J. Hunsecker.

CAPTAIN

Well, that's who it is. He wants you to come over to his house right away.

SIDNEY
(*on the move*)
Gentlemen, duty calls, and the best of friends must part, right?

TEMPLE

Sidney, Al and I talked it over and we want you to handle our account.

SIDNEY
(*pulling away*)
One of you guys want a bread and butter account?
(*to Temple*)
You act like I was looking for you.

He hurries away.

DRINKER
(*calling after him*)
Hey, Sidney, why don't you take me along, maybe I'll rub his back a little for ya, huh?

DISSOLVE TO:

INT. HALLWAY. HUNSECKER'S APARTMENT – NIGHT

The elevator door opens and Sidney steps out. He crosses to the door of the apartment, presses the buzzer. No response. Now he notices something that had escaped him before: the door is not quite shut. He pushes it open, goes inside.

INT. HUNSECKER'S APARTMENT

The apartment appears empty. Only one light is lit; the place is eerie. Sidney goes into the main living room, camera panning with him. Something chills him. He calls softly: 'J. J.?' He goes to the study, sees nobody there, keeps wandering until he comes to the half-open door to Susan's bedroom. He pushes the door open tentatively, looks in.

INT. BEDROOM

The bed has been slept in, but is unoccupied. The room is empty. The curtains of the open window onto the terrace are blowing. Sidney appears disturbed.

EXT. TERRACE

Susan is out on the terrace, at the parapet, looking down. She is half-undressed, wearing only a slip under the fur coat draped over her shoulders. She is in deep distress.

INT. BEDROOM

Sidney goes into the room, calls out a tentative: 'Susie?' Now he sees her
on the terrace, is dismayed, steps back as she comes into the room.

                    SIDNEY
                (nervously)
What are you doing out there at this time of the night?
        (he retreats outside the room as she comes toward him)
Uh . . . the door was open. Where's J. J.?

                    SUSAN
        (in a dead voice, standing in the bedroom doorway)
He isn't here . . .

                    SIDNEY
Well, I got a message to come over.

                    SUSAN
Did you?

                    SIDNEY
                (uneasily)
Well, well . . . if he isn't here I . . .

                    SUSAN
Mr D'Angelo phoned . . .

                    SIDNEY
Yeah?

                    SUSAN
About Steve . . .
                (voice breaking)
I went down . . . down . . . down to the hospital, but they
wouldn't let me in.

                    SIDNEY
                (cautiously)
It's all about town about Dallas? How is he?

INT. OUTER ROOM

Susan comes forward out of the bedroom, moving like a somnambulist, her voice filled with despair.

> SUSAN
>
> They wouldn't let me in . . . But I gave Steve up. Why did you and J. J. do it?

Sidney looks at her tensely, protests a little too loudly.

> SIDNEY
>
> What are you talking about? Who gives you the right to talk like that?

> SUSAN
> *(with damaging simplicity)*
>
> Don't bother to lie, Sidney. I don't care anymore.

Sidney puts on an air of tolerant sympathy, moves toward her.

> SIDNEY
>
> Look, Susie, you're very upset so I'm not gonna argue with you. Feeling sorry for yourself is not gonna help. Why don't you go to bed and get a good night's sleep, huh?

> SUSAN
>
> I'm sorry about Steve, not myself. I'm sorry about my brother . . .
> *(she faces him)*
> And I'm sorry about you, too, Sidney . . . Because you're going down with the ship . . .

> SIDNEY
>
> What ship?

> SUSAN
> *(indicating herself)*
>
> *This* ship. Don't you know how my brother is going to see you after tonight? You're going to be the man who drove his beloved little sister to suicide . . .

Shaken, Sidney forces a laugh. Probably she's bluffing. But he can't be certain. He tries to banish the threat from his mind with ridicule.

You know, Susie, I've heard this woman-talk before. Why
don't you start growing up, huh? Start thinking with your
head instead of your hips . . .
(goes to the bar, pours himself a drink)
By the way, I got nothing against women thinking with their
hips, that's their nature. Just like it's a man's nature to go out
and hustle and get the things he wants . . .

Susan's continued silence is getting to him. Anger creeps into his voice.

SIDNEY

Susie, look at yourself. You're nineteen years old, just a kid,
and you're falling apart at the seams. You tiptoe around on
those bird legs of yours, nervous and incompetent, with a
fatality for doing wrong, picking wrong, and giving up even
before you start to fight . . .

*Susan breaks, rushes into her bedroom, closes the door and locks it
against Sidney's attempt to push his way in.*

(at the door)
Wait a minute. It's the truth and the truth hurts . . .

*He walks away, sets his glass down, talks loudly toward the closed door,
trying to banish his growing anxiety.*

Come around some night when I'm not writing your
brother's column and I'll revise that delicate outlook of life
. . . To give credit where credit is due, Susie, that body of
yours deserves a better fate than tumbling off some
terrace . . .

SUSAN IN BEDROOM

She has taken off the fur coat, is wearing only her slip.

SIDNEY OUTSIDE OF CLOSED DOOR

SIDNEY
Susie, a bed is the best friend a girl ever had. Pleasant
dreams . . .

> (*puts his ear to the door, hears nothing*)
> Hey, now, don't be no square, don't do anything stupid . . .
> (*knocks on the door, rattles the knob*)
> Susie?

Alarmed, he rushes toward another entrance to the terrace.

EXT. TERRACE

Susan is moving swiftly from the bedroom across the terrace to the parapet to throw herself off. Sidney dashes onto the terrace and seizes her just as she is about to go over the edge.

                        SIDNEY
> Susie! . . .

She fights to go over. They struggle, and finally he overcomes her, and drags her back into the bedroom.

INT. BEDROOM

Susan is on the floor. Sidney is gasping for breath.

                        SIDNEY
> Are you crazy? Are you outta your mind?

He reaches down, pulls her up to a standing position. She cries out, pushes him away, falls across the bed, sobbing. He looks down at her desperately.

> What do you think your brother would say if I told him you tried a thing like that?

He goes to the bedroom door, opens it halfway, saying:

> I'll get you a drink . . .

                        SUSAN
                        (*cries*)
> Oh, go away!

Sidney pauses, noticing the open door to the terrace. Quickly he goes over to it, closes it, and approaches the bed.

SIDNEY
(*soothingly*)
Susie, look, I'm sorry . . .

Shooting through the open bedroom door, we see Hunsecker, just arrived, taking off his hat, approaching the sound of voices in the bedroom.

SIDNEY
(*voice-over*)
. . . If I said anything . . . Or did anything to hurt you . . .

SUSAN
(*voice-over; an angry cry*)
Get out of here!

Sidney is bending over Susan, saying: 'I did it –' He stops, straightens up as he sees Hunsecker coming in. Hunsecker approaches the bed.

HUNSECKER
It's all right, Susie. I'm here.
(*sits down on the bed, pats her*)
Take it easy, dear.

SIDNEY
(*trying to explain*)
J. J., Susie wasn't –

HUNSECKER
Calm yourself, dear. Now don't worry.

OUTER ROOM AND BEDROOM

Nervously, Sidney walks out of the bedroom, pauses outside the open doorway. Inside the bedroom, Hunsecker rises, gets Susie's robe and helps her into it.

HUNSECKER
Put this on, Susan.

He comes out of the bedroom, glances briefly at Sidney as he takes off his topcoat.

SIDNEY
(*carefully*)

J. J., it's lucky I came right over after I got your message. I got
here as quickly as I could, but . . .

HUNSECKER
(*turns to him*)

What message?
(*Sidney is speechless*)
Well, what message?

SIDNEY
(*trying to recover*)

Well, be that as it may, someone called me . . .
(*looks off, sees Susan getting to her feet*)
It's just lucky I got your message and came over here in
time . . .

HUNSECKER
(*sharply*)

Why?

SIDNEY

J. J., Susie was so depressed she tried to kill herself.

HUNSECKER
(*icily*)

Depressed? About what?

SIDNEY

Because she heard the news about Dallas . . .

*Within the bedroom, Susan is seen coming closer to the doorway,
listening.*

HUNSECKER

What news about Dallas?

Sidney is taken aback, becomes aware of Susan's presence, recovers.

SIDNEY

Oh, uh, I took it for granted, J. J., that you heard about it
around town. You're not gonna like this but they picked him
up on a marijuana rap.

156

HUNSECKER
(*with sudden menace*)
And is that why you put your hands on my sister?

*Stunned, Sidney backs away into the bedroom as Hunsecker slowly
comes in after him.*

SIDNEY
J. J., please . . . Susie tried to throw herself off the terrace . . .
(*goes to the terrace door, but it's closed*)
Susie, tell him the truth!
(*Hunsecker looks at her. She stays silent*)
Tell him!
(*Hunsecker moves at him*)
J. J., please, look, I can explain! . . .
(*Hunsecker strikes him savagely*)
J. J.! . . .

*Hunsecker smashes Sidney in the face again and again with violent fury
as Susan looks on, horrified. She finally grabs Hunsecker's arm.*

SUSAN
Stop! . . . Stop! . . . Stop! . . .

SIDNEY
(*blurts it out*)
*You're defending your sister, you big phony! Didn't you tell me to
get Kello? Didn't you –*

*He stops short, suddenly realizing what he has just said in Susan's
presence. Her expression freezes. Hunsecker's face becomes a mask.
There is a long, dreadful silence. Then Hunsecker steps back to Susan's
side, speaks quietly.*

HUNSECKER
Susie, just as I know he's lying about your attempted suicide,
you know he's lying about me. But we can't leave it like this,
can we . . .
(*he starts out of the bedroom*)
I suggest you go to bed, dear.

157

INT. LIVING-ROOM

Hunsecker comes out of the bedroom, goes quickly to the telephone, picks it up and starts to dial a number.

IN THE BEDROOM

Sidney looks at Susan.

> SIDNEY
>
> You're growing up . . .
>> (*starts away*)
>
> Cute.

He comes out of the bedroom, looks off toward Hunsecker at the phone. Within the bedroom, Susan can be seen beginning preparations to leave.

> HUNSECKER
>> (*off-screen*)
>
> Sergeant? This is J. J. Hunsecker. Let me talk to Lieutenant Kello . . .

IN THE LIVING ROOM

Sidney hurries toward the front door as:

> HUNSECKER
>> (*at phone*)
>
> Hello, Harry? I'm sorry to bother you, kid, but a bad mistake has been made . . .

> SIDNEY
>> (*turns*)
>
> J. J., you've got such contempt for people it makes you stupid!
>> (*Hunsecker looks at him*)
>
> You didn't beat those kids! You – you lost her! You'll never get her back!

> HUNSECKER
>> (*to phone*)
>
> Harry, Sidney Falco planted that stuff on Dallas . . . Jealousy . . . Behind my back he was trying to make my sister . . .

SIDNEY
(*at the open front door*)
That fat cop can break my bones, but he'll never stop me
from telling what I know!

THE FOYER

Sidney hurries out to the elevator, presses the down button.

INT. LIVING ROOM

HUNSECKER
(*at phone*)
He's leaving right now.

*He hangs up, sees Susan emerging from the bedroom. She is dressed in a
suit and hat, carries a small suitcase.*

Where do you think you're going?

Susan looks at him, starts away. He goes around her, blocks her path.

SUSAN
(*quietly*)
I'm leaving. I'm going to Steve.

She goes past him to the front door. He hurries after her.

HUNSECKER
No you're not. You're going into the hands of a good
psychoanalyst. You tried to kill yourself tonight.

SUSAN
(*turns, looks at him*)
Yes . . . I'd rather be dead than living with you.

*Hunsecker stares at her. She goes to the door, opens it. He moves to her
side.*

SUSAN
For all the things you've done, J. J., I know I should hate
you . . .
(*she looks at him*)
But I don't. I pity you.

160

She walks out. He stands with head bowed, at the half-open door. We see her step into the elevator.

EXT. DUFFY SQUARE — NIGHT

In a high angle long shot, Sidney is seen moving across the square, away from camera. A police squad car pulls up in foreground long enough for Harry Kello to get out, then speeds out of the shot to go around and cut off Sidney on the other side, as Kello follows him.

SIDNEY

Comes up toward camera, sees something ahead, comes to a wary halt.

SQUAD CAR

Braking to a stop, door swinging open.

SIDNEY

Backs away, turns, looks behind him.

HARRY KELLO

Smiles slightly as he closes in on Sidney.

SIDNEY

Reacts with dismay.

BESIDE THE SQUAD CAR

Another detective is moving into position.

LOW ANGLE LONG SHOT. THE SQUARE

Shooting past the back of the detective, we hear the crack of Kello's fists on Sidney's jaw, then, as the detective in foreground moves aside, we see Kello beyond, wiping his knuckles with a handkerchief as he stands over Sidney's writhing body on the sidewalk. Kello gestures to the other detective.

CLOSER ANGLE

Kello finishes wiping his hands, puts the handkerchief in his pocket, leans down over his victim, is joined by the other detective, and together they start to carry the limp form away.

LONG SHOT

The two cops drag Sidney Falco's body across Duffy Square as pigeons circle overhead.

EXT. ENTRANCE TO HUNSECKER'S BUILDING

Susan comes out of the entrance onto Broadway, her small suitcase in her hand. She pauses on the sidewalk for a moment, glancing about. The sky is growing brighter.

EXT. HUNSECKER'S TERRACE

Hunsecker comes out onto the terrace, moves forward to the parapet and looks off, with anguish on his face.

EXT. BROADWAY

Susan moves into a patch of early morning sunlight, then walks away toward a new day.

Afterword

For all the cynicism it portrays, *Sweet Smell of Success* is a film directed by an idealist, a perfectionist and an innovator. In 1981, when I was seventeen and in my first week of art school, I met Sandy Mackendrick. He was a giant presence at Cal Arts. Students, professors, deans, cafeteria workers, everyone was in awe of him. Though seventy years old, Sandy was a strapping, broad-chested genius with little patience for ignorance and even less for talent unmarried to discipline. Fresh out of suburban high school, my only reference for a man like this was the John Houseman I had seen on seventies TV as Professor Kingsfield in *The Paper Chase*.

I had a pile of Super 8 films under my arm and was desperate for Sandy to become my mentor. I watched all his movies (*The Man in the White Suit, The Maggie, The Ladykillers, Whisky Galore* and *Sweet Smell of Success,* to name a few), but he wanted nothing to do with such a youngster. I was persistent. I forced him to watch my collection of shorts. I will never be as proud of anything as changing his mind that day.

As I sit here, over fifteen years later, I profoundly miss Alexander Mackendrick. He taught me more craft than I could articulate, but beyond that, he showed me how hard one had to work to make even a decent film. He demonstrated – on a daily basis – the sharp elbows, passionate heart and evangelical tongue required to defend and nurture innovative projects.

The innovation of *Sweet Smell* is often credited to Ernest Lehman's courageous portrayal – in his original novelette and screenplay – of the underbelly of the post-war American media machine. But the dazzling achievement of the film springs not merely from its politics – many mediocre films of the fifties took on important political concerns – but from its swirlingly brilliant screen-narrative and language – verbal and visual. Sandy supervised all the rewrites on the film. When Ernest Lehman fell ill, Sandy chose Clifford Odets to do the rewrites. The collaboration of these three continued through production.

'What I really enjoyed about working with Clifford,' said Sandy about Odets, 'was his craft in the *structuring* of scenes. One of Odets' passions was chamber music. Particularly string quartets. He took great delight in the craft of the composers who knew how to interweave the five "voices" of the instruments so that each has its own "line" throughout the work, each distinct from the others but all of them combining to make sure the whole was greater than just the sum of the parts.'

Mackendrick's office at Cal Arts was adorned with nearly thirty framed aphorisms that ran the circumference of the room. They were rendered in a faux needlepoint style (Sandy was a wonderful illustrator, as shown by his storyboards printed on the following pages), and they said things such as:

1 A character who is intelligent and dramatically interesting THINKS AHEAD.

2 EXPOSITION can only be dramatic when it emerges in the context of DRAMATIC CONFLICT.

3 A FOIL CHARACTER is a figure invented to ask the questions to which your audience needs answers. (*It may be more important to have the questions clearly asked than to provide an immediate answer.*)

4 In movies what is SAID is less effective than what is SEEN HAPPENING.

5 The 'action' of the ANTAGONIST(S) is often more important to the structure of the PLOT than the intentions of the PROTAGONIST.

6 Don't expect audiences to register the names of characters mentioned in the dialogue but not shown on the screen.

There were no aphorisms about eyelines or blocking or camera placement. Sandy was a director who built his films from the script up. He believed a film's value and style, its jazz and its meaning, all stemmed from the screenplay. And he knew, as most decent film-makers (but few outside the process) do, that a script is more than a libretto of zippy dialogue. It is *what is seen happening* in *what order* to *whom, where.*

166

To that end, I want to examine the front end of *Sweet Smell* through the introduction of J. J. Hunsecker (Burt Lancaster) at the Twenty-One Club. Of the selected aphorisms above, the first five are all clearly implemented in these sequences. Ernest Lehman's exposition in *Sweet Smell* is artfully dispensed (given the bewildering world of the press agent); we are told only what we must know to survive the current scene.

From the moment Sidney Falco (Tony Curtis) is introduced, we see a man in crisis. The exact nature of this crisis is indistinct, but it clearly emanates from a columnist named J. J. Hunsecker. Even without understanding the exact nature of Sidney's profession, we see in his artful maneuvers that he is clearly a man who thinks ahead (Rule #1). We (the audience) are continually catching up with him. We learn about this world as a) Sidney spars with frustrated clients, b) responds to the romantic whinings of his assistant, c) slinks his way toward Susan and Steve, maneuvering past Steve's manager and a cigarette girl desperate for a favor – both characters to be used effectively later – and d) escorts Susan home, discovering her engagement. Each dollop of exposition religiously follows Rule # 2. Every scene has a present purpose and conflict, as well as serving to dispense more and more backstory.

Sidney's assistant is the first 'foil character' introduced (Rule #3) and asks him *'Why is Mr Hunsecker trying to squeeze your livelihood away? What do you stand this kind of treatment for?'* – this charged with the lingering feeling that Sidney has taken comfort in her 'meaty arms' in the past. He responds with a passion-charged monologue about getting *'up there where everything's balmy'* and no one snaps their fingers and says, *'Hey – kid – rack up the balls.'*

However, the essential load of exposition (just what *is* a press agent? What does Sidney Falco do for a living, and why is he necessary?) is denied us. Without it, we (the audience) are living fully through Rule #4. We watch both the machiavellian and the ass-kissing *behaviors* of a press agent without much explanation or comment upon the rationale behind them. It makes the movie smart. Lehman and Odets make us work a little. Something we experience rarely these days. In fact, in this age of intensive audience previews where everything needs to be fully comprehensible at every moment (unless you are making a mystery), this kind of slow-spooned exposition is nearly impossible to get through the system.

And this is where a whole second tier of structural brilliance comes into play. Sandy chose to defy his own rule (#6). But to our benefit. For the first twenty minutes of the film, everyone is talking relentlessly about J. J. Hunsecker with nearly religious fear and respect. But he goes unseen.

Sweet Smell's build-up to the introduction of J. J. Hunsecker at the Twenty-One yields one of the great character introductions in the history of film. Lehman, Odets and Mackendrick boldly chose to force us to deal with J. J. in every possible perceptual way before introducing him as a live human presence on-screen. Equipped (as he was) with an awareness that he was breaking one of his own cardinal rules, Sandy compensated for the gamble with a breathless pace. He knew Hunsecker was being played by one of the biggest stars of the day and the longer his arrival was delayed, the more it would build suspense and appreciation of J. J.'s supreme status in the world of the story.

1 In the very *first image* of the film we see J. J.'s name and face slathered on the side of the newspaper trucks leaving the warehouse.
2 In the first scene, we see J. J. Hunsecker's likeness on the banner atop his column as Sidney reads it with disgust at a hot dog stand.
3 We then follow Sidney through a night's work – all the time hearing J. J.'s name invoked with fear and/or reverence.
4 Sidney goes to the Twenty-One and asks 'Is he here?' A maître d' nods and we see a table in the dining-room with a man's back to us (J. J.). Ever thinking ahead (Rule #1), Sidney measures his moves. He chooses *not* to plunge into the club and confront J. J. Instead, the brilliant indulgence of this tease is tested one more time as –
5 Sidney calls J. J. on a house phone. It is now, for the first time that we hear the sinister voice of Hunsecker. 'You're dead son, get yourself buried.' Sidney now, with some hesitation, marches into the dining-room where –
6 Lancaster (J. J.) is finally unveiled. Sandy worked this first image of Hunsecker out very carefully with James Wong Howe

(the cinematographer), who top-lit Hunsecker in his horn rims so that his head resembled a skull. J. J. tells a waiter to have Sidney escorted out – until, that is, Sidney (thinking ahead once again) lets Hunsecker know that his sister is about to become engaged.

This is brilliant film-making. The movie up to this point has been dancing through a dark parade of major and minor characters. There is no one left to introduce. We have met *everybody*. Only J. J. remained veiled. And no one previously introduced failed to discuss J. J., the great unseen monster. Lehman claims this choice came from his subconscious, without planning. Many bold ideas come to a writer quietly and without fanfare – a feather falling in the night – but when they fly in the face of accepted practice, it requires real courage for the writer and the team that follows to maintain the bold choice and avoid backsliding.

This unique first act structure is not merely a stylistic device. The holding back of J. J. until all other story forces have been set in place (all of these plot lines reactive to his power), is what *makes* J. J. Hunsecker so impressive upon his introduction. It is not just Lancaster's searing portrayal. It is not merely Howe's cadaverous lighting. It is not simply the sparkling dialogue of Lehman/Odets, nor Sandy's swinging dark camera and furious blocking. J. J.'s power comes from the film's core architecture. The sum that is greater than the parts. Hunsecker's introduction is the arrival of the missing link. Once we confront him, we retroactively understand everything that preceded this moment. And the movie structurally unites with its own setting and theme. We have not been merely told that the world of the press agent is a dark labyrinth, we have been *shown it* (Rule #4); we have felt, first-hand, the humiliating scramble for the access to power.

And who is at J. J.'s table? Not only a talent manager, Manny Davis (expected), and a pretty actress (expected) but a United States senator who is apparently trying to get his 'Jersey' mistress (the 'actress') a gig through J. J.'s influence. With such a table setting any confusion over the level of J. J.'s power (or 'the system') is quite literally demonstrated. What might be another movie's authority figure (senator) is witnessed groveling before J. J.'s power to anoint. Says J. J., at the scene's climax, 'God willing, Senator, you might want to be President one day. Yet here you are, out in the open, where any hep cat can see that this one (Manny) is toting around that one (actress) *for you*. Are we friends or what?'

Dialogue – no matter how clever or poetic – plays like this only when the architecture of the film supports it. The elements (narrative, performance, visual, verbal, musical) have to *dance*. The crafters of this film – Lehman, Odets and Mackendrick were not just smart, they were very smart and they gave the senator an additional purpose here. The senator asks Sidney to explain what it is he does for a living – what is a press agent? And so it is that we finally (Rule #3) get a foil to ask the question that we've been dying to understand. What exactly is Sidney doing? And instead of a merely verbal response we also get to *see* the relationship on the other side of the table, between a press agent (Sidney would now be called a publicist) and an influential columnist. Sidney sits to J. J.'s side, just a bit behind him. It is immediately understood. They may snipe at each other, but Sidney is an ally, a junior officer in 'the war'.

There is a Shakespearean aura to this film. It is rare in modern movies to follow characters who are so irredeemable and ambitious. But as we see in Sandy's Rule #5, antagonists drive a story. And this story's particularly intense drive comes from the fact that our central characters are conniving, cunning, methodical, lying – in short, innately evil. Throughout the film, there is a tenuous dance between elaborate scene constructions and economical story-telling – we move from location to location, club to TV studio (an amazing scene of five-step manipulation) to club to office without confusion, just momentum. Notice the beautiful symmetry of the two cigarette girl and Herbie Temple scenes.

The spiral toward the climactic triple-cross is a beautiful narrative sculpture of bluffs, lies and counter lies with the seemingly innocent Susan proving to be every bit up to the twisted methods of her adversaries. According to Sandy, this final conflict in the penthouse was the source of several battles between the producers (including the star, Burt Lancaster) and the writer/director team. Odets rewrote it several times. Sandy shot it twice and recalled staging it in such a complex series of movements and linking shots that – should the producers seize the movie – would make it impossible for them to cut the footage any other way.

Like many innovative masterpieces, *Sweet Smell of Success* was unappreciated when it premièred. Sandy believed there were several reasons for this, 'One, I suspect, was that many of the reviewers, particularly those from the Hearst papers, were outraged by what they felt – rightly – was a pretty savage attack on one branch of their profession, the press agents and gossip columnists, believing that the central figure was a libelous (portrayal) of a very famous journalist who was extremely powerful during the era of the blacklist. Another may have been because it offended the fans of Tony Curtis who had, up till that point, appeared only in quite sympathetic roles, the juvenile lead in light romantic comedies. Tony himself had accepted the role enthusiastically, but the movie-going public was clearly unprepared for the shock of seeing one of their favorite young leading men presented as a reptilian figure who, in the end, emerges as even more corrupt than his villainous associate played by Burt Lancaster. There were some commentators, indeed, who saw the whole subject as an attack of the 'American Way of Life' and the 'success ethos'.

I find Sandy's point about Curtis particularly interesting as I had a similar experience on *CopLand*. Instead of his archetypal super hero role, Sylvester Stallone portrayed a more hesitant, damaged character. In previews, we experienced a 'disconnect' between Stallone and his core audience. We made some attempts to correct for it but it didn't change the reality that the fan base of an iconic star can get frustrated if their hero takes a severe departure from type. When one Rambo fan in a focus group was asked how he would describe *CopLand* to his friends, he replied concisely, 'I'd tell 'em that Stallone's a fat wimp.'

Beyond the 'glamorous-stars-playing-flawed characters' problem, there is yet another issue that certainly hurt *Sweet Smell's* box-office prospects. This is not a story about a dark hero changing his ways (redemption), this is a film about his *undoing* (tragedy). This is mitigated only by the triumph of a second tier love story. Some find the film depressing. However, when you mention *Sweet Smell* to many film-makers, it brings a profound grin. Despite Sidney's tragic end, there is such structural genius and moment to moment wit and humor, not to mention the pleasure derived from watching Susan (the depressive waif) outmaneuvre Sidney and J. J., that *Sweet Smell's* proud swagger overwhelms the story's dark outcome for Sidney. One could even mount a decent argument that Susan is, in fact, the movie's true (but rarely seen) protagonist.

Barry Levinson made fond references to *Sweet Smell* in both *Rain Man* where a clip from the film plays on a television in a hotel room Cruise and Hoffman are staying, and in *Diner* where a supporting character continually spouts J. J. Hunsecker dialogue. Levinson told me he thought *Sweet Smell* might have been overlooked, both at its initial release and over time, partly because its setting and characters were so hard to sell to an audience. 'I mean, I just happened to see it. I just walked in the theater. But I was absolutely knocked out by the movie. What got me was the dialogue. There was such a stylistic naturalism. It was amazing.'

Martin Scorsese told me he also remembered seeing *Sweet Smell* upon its initial release at the Astor in New York City in 1959. 'The thing we loved about it was the toughness. It was such a tough film. The way it was written. It was vibrant, alive. The images of New York, the location work were all brilliant. And of course, the amazing performances. We loved Tony Curtis. It was a world of operators I knew very well – except of course I never knew anyone like J. J. Hunsecker.'

I mentioned *Sweet Smell* to Paul Thomas Anderson because I thought I had heard one of Chico Hamilton's jazz pieces from *Sweet Smell* in *Boogie Nights*. He confirmed the 'quote' and also said that when he was in England a reporter asked him what he thought might be the greatest screenplay of all time. He thought a second and said, 'You know, I think I'd pick *Sweet Smell of Success*.' The reporter was stunned, 'That's amazing, James Mangold was here last week and he said the same thing.'

Of course I did. While, in truth, one could point to a bias on my part (as my teacher made the film) – and it can get plain ridiculous, even nauseating, making 'best of' lists in any category – I can't diminish the inspiration I have gotten from this film. Lehman crafted a truly original story, a great morality tale. Odets danced with some of the scene structures and dialogue till it sang. Elmer Bernstein's score was swank, brassy, bold and moving. 'No one would let you get away with a score like that today,' Bernstein told me. 'To get that out in front – people would cringe.' James Wong Howe's brooding, smoky, low-angle black and white photography was revolutionary, as was his low-light location shooting of Manhattan. Burt Lancaster was maniacal and controlled. Tony Curtis leapt headlong against the currents of his 'boy with the ice-cream face' career and made arguably the greatest performance of his life.

This synergy, these bold choices and collaborations, all these musical strands coming together in one remarkable film must have something to do with the brilliance and leadership of the conductor. And because I knew Sandy, I know it did. And because I have worked in this business, I also know the answer to the next question. *Why didn't he make ten more films like this?*

In truth, Sandy made a dazzling run of films in the UK at Ealing which culminated with his arrival in America to make *Sweet Smell of Success*. However, his emigration (not really an emigration as he was Boston-born) also marked the beginning of a difficult period.

I asked Elmer Bernstein about the environment on the set of *Sweet Smell*. 'I wasn't privy to everything, but the combination of people on that movie – Harold Hecht, Burt Lancaster, Cliff Odets who was crazy – good crazy, but crazy – it was a snake pit. There was a cultural distance between Burt and Sandy. It was like Sandy's heart beat at a different rate. Burt was really scary. He was a dangerous guy. He had a short fuse. He was very physical. You thought you might get punched out.* I mean, I was in the projection room once and I saw Burt chasing someone around. Sandy was a lovely man. It was a miracle that he finished that film. In fact, I think that film is what finished Sandy – as a film-maker.'

The same perfectionism and vision that can yield a brilliant film can also assist in the cooling of a career. One can become a 'problem' director. Particularly in the absence of Oscars or dollars. Sandy did not give up making movies after *Sweet Smell*, in fact he signed on to direct another Hill/Hecht/Lancaster project (*The Devil's Disciple*). However, Bernstein was right, this was a turning

---

* Ernest Lehman adds: 'At one point Lancaster muttered to me, "I oughta punch you in the jaw right here and now." To which I replied, "Go ahead, Burt, I need the money." '

point for Mackendrick. And the projects to follow were often troubled.

Burt Lancaster fired Sandy from *The Devil's Disciple*. He was taking too long. 'Sandy told us not to worry, but after shooting a week we had only two days of film,' said Lancaster, 'so we called him in and let him go. It's ironic that his two days of the film are the best in the picture.'

Then, Edward G. Robinson had a stroke on *The Boy Who Was Ten Feet Tall*, forcing Sandy to shoot half the film with a dubbed photo double. Sandy prepared to shoot *The Guns of Navarone* (he performed uncredited rewrites and designed the film – his beautiful sketches of the great gun in the mountain were all over his office) but left the project a few weeks before production. *A High Wind in Jamaica* (with Anthony Quinn) was not a hit. And a stunt man tragically died on his final feature film, a comedy, *Don't Make Waves*.

Upon these misfortunes, was an atmosphere of contraction and confusion in the film business (it was the mid-sixties and TV was making everyone scared and drying up production). Sandy directed some television – *The Defenders*. In declining health, he contracted emphysema. When offered the chance to run a film school, he jumped. I caught him twenty years later.

Sweet Smell of Success is one of the great American films. Ask Martin Scorsese. Ask Paul Thomas Anderson. Ask Barry Levinson. Ask me. I have watched it a dozen times. I will surely see it again soon. It is a miracle of craft and passion and it was directed by my great teacher. I am supremely proud to have touched his genius and his heart.

James Mangold, 1998

Alexander Mackendrick and Tony Curtis